*English for Business
and Professional
Examinations*

Other Titles in the Business Studies Series:

Edwards: THE FRAMEWORK OF ECONOMICS

Gregory & Ward: STATISTICS FOR BUSINESS STUDIES

Marsh: OUTLINES OF ENGLISH LAW

Shafto: COMMERCE: STRUCTURE AND PRACTICE

Shafto: STUDY NOTES ON COMMERCE

English for Business and Professional Examinations

Second edition

Neil Butterworth, M.A.

Senior Lecturer, Edinburgh College of Commerce

McGRAW-HILL Book Company (UK) Limited

London · New York · St Louis · San Francisco · Auckland · Beirut
Bogotá · Düsseldorf · Johannesburg · Lisbon · Lucerne · Madrid
Mexico · Montreal · New Delhi · Panama · Paris · San Juan · São Paulo
Singapore · Sydney · Tokyo · Toronto

Published by McGraw-Hill Book Company (UK) Limited
MAIDENHEAD · BERKSHIRE · ENGLAND

07 094297 8

Copyright © 1967, 1974 McGraw-Hill Book Company (UK) Limited. All rights reserved. No part of this publication may be reproduced, stored in a retrieval system, or transmitted, in any form or by any means, electronic, mechanical, photocopying, recording, or otherwise, without the prior permission of McGraw-Hill Book Company (UK) Limited.

8 9 10 11 A.P. 80/98
PRINTED AND BOUND IN GREAT BRITAIN

Preface

In business communication, clarity and conciseness of expression are of paramount importance. Often, time is wasted, with a consequent loss of money, through misunderstandings or queries which arise as a result of poor communication. Pressure of time is usually the cause of such problems. In the business world, work has to be done quickly, with little or no opportunity for revision. For this reason, a student planning a business career must develop an efficient communication technique which will combine speed with clarity and conciseness.

In order to achieve this, the student needs constant practice in those things which he will need to do in the business world: practice in formulating and expressing ideas clearly, in interpreting and summarizing written communication, in writing business letters and reports, and in speaking effectively.

Because I believe that in training for a business career the emphasis should be on practice rather than on study, I have written *English for Business and Professional Examinations*. My own criticism of the majority of existing English textbooks is that they contain insufficient exercise material. I have limited the instructional material in the text to essentials so that there is room for copious exercises.

All too often the student of English sees the examination as an end in itself and not as an integral part of his training for a business career. I have endeavoured to show the significance in the business world of the various disciplines imposed by the examinations. After all, what is précis writing but training for summarizing, which is so vital in the busy office of today?

The extended essay for the OND and ONC courses in Business Studies has not been overlooked. Suggestions and hints on writing and presenting an essay of this type have been included in the chapter on writing essays.

I have also included a chapter on discussion work for practical use in class teaching, and as a training in effective oral communication.

English for Business and Professional Examinations provides a basic course in English for students preparing for the OND and ONC in Business Studies; the Clerical Examination and Diploma in Municipal Administration of the Local Government Examinations Board; the Shorthand Typist's Certificate Stages II and III of the Royal Society of Arts; the Private Secretary's Certificate and Diploma of the London Chamber of Commerce; the Part I examination of the Institute of Bankers; the Intermediate examination of the Institute of Chartered Secretaries and Administrators; the Intermediate Part I examination of the Building Society Institute; the Graduateship examination of the Institute of Transport; the Intermediate examination of the Institute of Export; the Foremanship and Supervision examination of the City and Guilds of London Institute; the Associate Part I examination of the Savings Bank Institute; and the Introductory examination of the Chartered Insurance Institute.

Since I believe that it is imperative for every student preparing for one of these examinations to have a copy of the syllabus and past examination papers, the full address of each board is given in Appendix I. Only by studying the syllabus and past examination papers will the student be able to discover the exact nature of the paper and the type of question set.

In the case of the professional bodies, it is necessary for every candidate to be a registered member of the institute concerned before entering for the examination. It is the individual responsibility of each student to be certain that he is qualified in this respect.

Acknowledgements. I should like to express my thanks to the following writers and publishers for their permission to reproduce material: the Right Honourable Fred Lee, M.P.; Mr. Arthur Seldon; B.B.C. Publications; the Public Trustee; Constable & Co. Ltd.; Mrs. Laura Huxley and Chatto & Windus Ltd.; the S.C.M. Press Ltd.; The Controller of Her Majesty's Stationery Office; William Collins & Co. Ltd.; Cassell & Co. Ltd.; Methuen & Co. Ltd.; Medica Social Publications; and Thames & Hudson Ltd. My thanks are also due to the following organizations: the Society of Authors; A. P. Watt & Son; the Arts Council of Great Britain; Blackwood, Morton & Sons, Ltd.; Manchester Liners Ltd.; the National Provincial Bank Ltd.; Spicers Limited; and the National Trust. I must also thank the following periodicals and newspapers: *The Countryman*; *The Daily Telegraph*; *The Guardian*; *The London Evening News*; *The New Daily*; *The Sunday Times*; *The Times*; and *The Times Educational Supplement*. I am indebted to the following examining bodies for their permission to reproduce past examination questions: the Chartered Institute of Secretaries; the Corporation of Secretaries; the Institute of Bankers; the Institute of Transport; the London Chamber of Commerce; the Local Government Examinations Board; and the Royal Society of Arts.

NEIL BUTTERWORTH

Contents

Preface

1. Using words effectively — 1
2. Using language effectively — 14
3. The mechanics of style — 26
4. Writing essays — 42
5. Interpreting written communication — 55
6. Summarizing written communication — 77
7. Writing business letters — 119
8. Business reports and meetings — 133
9. Effective speaking — 144

Appendix I. Addresses of examining boards — 160

Appendix II. Bibliography — 162

1. Using words effectively

The importance of a good vocabulary

Words are, to the speaker or writer, like paint to the artist. By using his paints skilfully, the artist can create a picture which conveys a message to those who look at it. By choosing his words carefully, the speaker or writer can also convey a picture to his listeners or readers. Obviously, the wider his choice of words, the more accurate is the picture which he can convey.

Always use a dictionary

To communicate effectively, you must become thoroughly familiar with your dictionary. Those who use words extensively—journalists, editors, business executives—keep a dictionary within easy reach, and use it often.

The first comprehensive dictionary of the English language was compiled by Dr. Samuel Johnson and published in 1755. His intention was to produce 'a dictionary by which the pronunciation of our language may be fixed, and its attainments facilitated; by which its purity may be preserved, its use ascertained, and its duration lengthened'.

As the work of one man, Dr. Johnson's dictionary was a remarkable achievement. It became the basis upon which all subsequent dictionaries have been built.

With the considerable advance in scholarship and linguistic research, it is now possible to classify almost every word in current usage. Dictionaries are now available which cover specialist subjects and include the numerous technical terms which are being constantly created, especially in the field of science.

In an authoritative dictionary, it is possible to discover a considerable range of information beyond the spelling and basic meaning of each word. Under most entries one can find the pronunciation, the special meaning of words in idiomatic phrases, figurative usage, grammatical function, other parts of speech derived from the word, and the etymological derivation.

You should possess a good-quality dictionary. A pocket edition will suffice for the general meaning and spelling of words, but the *Concise Oxford Dictionary*, *Webster's Dictionary* or one of equivalent standard ought to be readily available for reference.

Semantics... The meaning of words

A correct word is vital to effective communication. This is why a question which appears frequently in many English examination papers concerns the writing of sentences to show clearly the exact meaning of certain words. Such sentences must not only contain the word used correctly but should convey sufficient information to imply the meaning of the word by its context.

Let us suppose the word 'zealous' is to be used in a sentence to illustrate its meaning. 'He was a zealous pupil' gives no indication of the meaning of the word at all. It has been correctly used as an adjective, but beyond this the sentence is unsatisfactory.

The following sentence gives enough detail to suggest the meaning of the word 'zealous', without being itself a mere definition.

The zealous members of the Republican Party were canvassing the electors every evening for weeks before the election.

Sometimes you may be asked to explain as clearly as possible the meaning of a certain word. What is required is a definition, not a sentence which uses the word correctly.

A correct answer in this case for the word 'zealous' would be as follows:

Zealous means showing considerable fervour and enthusiasm for a cause.

You may be asked to differentiate between pairs of words. In this case the essential difference in meaning must be made clear. No credit is given for sentences which use the words correctly but do not indicate the difference in meaning.

It rained continuously during the night.
The mice ran continually across the floor of the room above.

In the above sentences, the words 'continuously' and 'continually' could be transposed with no apparent alteration in meaning. The context of each sentence must make it impossible for the two words to be interchangeable.

The car ran continuously for six hours before lack of petrol forced it to retire from the race.

As the clerk was continually late in the morning, the manager considered that he was too unreliable to be given promotion.

Perhaps the most exacting questions are those which ask you to define a noun. In order to do this, the noun must first be placed in its general category, and then separated from all the other items in that group. Things are usually described either by what they look like or by their function, or both. Definitions should be kept as simple as possible; if too much detail is included, numerous exceptions can arise.

A table is an article of furniture with a flat top and vertical supports.

Since a table is used for so many purposes it is not possible to include these in the definition. Although most tables have four legs, a table with more or less than four is still a table, so that the number of vertical supports is better omitted.

A spoon requires to be defined by both its appearance and its purpose in order that an adequate definition can be composed.

A spoon is an article of cutlery consisting of a shallow bowl and a handle, used for conveying food to the mouth.

One way to achieve variety in word usage is by the use of *synonyms*. A synonym is a word of identical or closely similar meaning to another word; for example, 'apt' is a synonym for 'suitable'. In

3

order to help you achieve this variety, exercises are often set which require the replacement of given words by synonyms. You must often be satisfied with words that have the closest possible meaning to those given, since there are only a few pairs of words which have precisely the same meaning in any context. Most words alter their meaning according to the context and specific usage.

Antonyms may also be used in order to achieve variety. An antonym is a word which means exactly the opposite of another word. For example, 'black' is an antonym for 'white'. Variety may be achieved by using the antonym in a negative phrase; for example, 'He had won so many races, that they all felt that he could not lose this one', rather than, 'He had won so many races, that they all felt he must win this one'.

Using foreign phrases

English is a language which has taken words and phrases from many other languages. Familiarize yourself with the following:

Latin phrases

ad hoc	arranged for a special purpose
ad infinitum	for ever
ad valorem	in proportion to the value
a fortiori	with stronger reason
a priori	deduced
bona fide	genuine, with good faith
circa	about (regarding dates)
data	facts known; given information
de facto	in fact
Deo volente	God willing
deus ex machina	the intervention of divine powers to solve difficulty
ex cathedra	from the highest authority
ex libris	bookplate (from the library of . . .)
ex officio	by virtue of office or position
ex parte	in the interests of one side only
in camera	in private (not in open court)
infra dig(*nitatem*)	unbecoming
in loco parentis	(acting) in place of a parent
in situ	in its proper or original place

inter alia	amongst other things
in toto	completely
ipso facto	by that very fact
locum tenens	temporary deputy for a doctor or clergyman
modus operandi	way a thing operates
modus vivendi	mode of living
multum in parvo	much contained in a small space
mutatis mutandis	with due alteration of detail
nem(ine) con(tradicente)	unanimously
ne plus ultra	highest point attainable
non sequitur	an illogical statement (which does not follow)
onus probandi	burden of proof
passim	to be found throughout the works of specified authors
per se	in itself, intrinsically
persona grata	acceptable person
prima facie	at first sight
pro forma	for the sake of form
pro rata	in proportion
pro tem(pore)	for the time being, temporarily
quasi	seemingly, in the manner of
quid pro quo	fair compensation
quorum	minimum number of people to constitute a meeting
sine die	(adjourned) indefinitely
sine qua non	indispensable condition
status quo	unchanged or original condition
stet	let it stand (cancel correction)
sub judice	under judicial consideration (and comment prohibited)
sub rosa	in confidence
ultra vires	beyond one's authority
viva voce	oral examination

French phrases

apropos	with regard to
bête noire	strong personal dislike
bon mot	witty remark
bon vivant	gourmand, lover of good food

carte blanche	full powers
chef d'œvre	masterpiece
coup de grâce	finishing stroke
coup d'état	revolution
débâcle	collapse, downfall (of a government)
de rigueur	required by etiquette
de trop	not required, unwelcome
double entendre	ambiguous expression
enfant terrible	revolutionary young man (especially in the arts)
en masse	all together
en passant	by the way
entrepreneur	a business organizer
esprit de corps	regard for honour
fait accompli	action completed and not worth arguing about
faux pas	an indiscreet blunder
gauche	tactless, socially awkward
hors de combat	out of action
impasse	position from which there is no escape
jeu d'esprit	a witty remark
laissez-faire	lack of government interference
noblesse oblige	privilege which entails responsibility
nom de plume	pen name, pseudonym
pièce de résistance	most important item
poste restante	Post Office department where letters are kept until collected
pot pourri	medley (musical or literary)
raison d'être	purpose which justifies a thing's existence
rapport	relationship
sans-souci	carefree
savoir faire	quickness of action, tact
soi disant	self-styled
tête-à-tête	private conversation
tour de force	feat of skill or strength
vis-à-vis	face to face
volte face	complete change of attitude

Saving your company's time

In the business world, you will come across many abbreviations. Since abbreviations save time and hence money, you should become familiar with the following:

Crown honours

B.E.M.	C.V.O.	K.B.E.	M.M.
C.B.	D.B.E.	K.C.B.	M.V.O.
C.B.E.	G.C.	K.C.M.G.	O.B.E.
C.H.	G.C.M.G.	K.C.V.O.	O.M.
C.M.G.	G.C.V.O.	M.B.E.	P.C.
C.S.I.	G.M.	M.C.	V.C.

Qualifications

A.C.I.S.	B.D.	D.D.	F.R.S.L.
A.C.A.	B.Ed.	D.Lit.	L.D.S.
A.M.I.C.E.	B.L.	D.Litt.	Ll.B.
A.M.I.E.E.	B.Litt.	D.Mus.	L.R.A.M.
A.M.I.Mech.E.	B.M.	D.Phil. (Ph.D.)	L.R.C.P.
A.R.I.B.A.	B.Mus. (Mus.B.)	D.Sc.	M.A.
A.R.C.O.	B.Sc.	Dunelm.	Oxon.
B.A.	Cantab.	F.R.C.O.	Q.C.
B.C.L.	D.C.L.	F.R.S.	R.A.
B.Com.			

English counties

Hants.	Leics.	Lincs.	Mx.
Oxon.	Salop.	Staffs.	Worcs.

American States

Ala.	Ia.	Mo.	Pa.
Alas.	Ill.	Mont.	R.I.
Ariz.	Ind.	N.C.	S.C.
Ark.	Kan.	N.Dak.	S.Dak.
Cal.	Ky.	Neb(r).	Tenn.
Colo.	La.	Nev.	Tex.
Conn.	L.I.	N.H.	Ut.
Dak.	Mass.	N.J.	Va.
D.C.	Md.	N.Mex.	Vt.
Del.	Me.	N.Y.	Wash.
Fla.	Mich.	O.	Wisc.
Ga.	Minn.	Okla.	W.Va.
Ha.	Miss.	Ore.	Wyo.
I.			

Organizations

A.A.	C.B.I.	N.A.T.O.	S.E.A.T.O.
B.B.C.	C.I.D.	N.C.B.	T.G.
B.E.A.	E.E.C.	N.H.S.	U.N.E.S.C.O.
B.M.A.	E.M.I.	N.S.P.C.C.	U.P.
B.O.A.C.	F.B.I.	P.L.A.	W.I.
B.P.	G.P.O.	R.A.C.	W.E.A.
B.R.	I.A.T.A.	R.A.D.A.	W.H.O.
B.S.A.	I.C.I.	R.H.S.	Y.H.A.
B.S.I.	I.M.F.	R.S.	Y.M.C.A.
B.U.P.	M.C.C.	R.S.P.C.A.	Y.W.C.A.

Unions

| A.E.U. | E.T.U. | N.A.L.G.O. | N.U.M. |
| N.U.S. | N.U.T. | T.G.W.U. | T.U.C. |

Miscellaneous

A.D.	G.M.T.	O.H.M.S.	R.C.
A.V.	H.M.S.	O.S.	R.D.C.
B.T.U.	I.Q.	O.T.	R.S.V.P.
C.	J.P.	P.A.Y.E.	S.R.N.
C. of E.	M.F.H.	P.M.G.	V.A.T.
Fahr.	O.E.D.	P.R.O.	V.I.P.

Commercial and secretarial terms

a/c	E. & O.E.	inst.	N.P.
caps	etc.	ital.	op. cit.
cf.	et seq.	l.c.	per pro
c.i.f.	ex. div.	Ltd.	pp.
Co.	fcp.	memo.	q.v.
c/o	f.o.b.	Messrs.	trs.
C.O.D.	f.o.r.	misc.	u.c.
Cr.	ibid.	MS.	ult.
cwt.	i/c	MSS	viz.
do.	id.	N.B.	vv.
Dr.	i.e.	n.d.	w.f.
dwt.	Inc.	nos.	wt.

Build a good vocabulary

Remember, a good vocabulary is an asset. Become vocabulary conscious. Be alert to new and different words; learn their meaning, their spelling, their correct usage. Here your dictionary can be an invaluable asset. Practise new words until they become familiar. Variety and precision in word usage are essential to effective communication in business.

EXERCISES

1. Give briefly the meaning of the following words and use each in a sentence.

acquiesce	altruistic	concession
actuary	ambivalent	condone
acumen	anachronism	confederate
affluent	analogy	consensus
aggravate	aridity	consolidate
alacrity	circumlocution	conspectus

contemporary	incongruity	plagiarism
contiguous	indict	plebiscite
criterion	indolent	posterity
deference	inertia	potentate
desultory	inimical	preponderance
diatribe	initiative	procrastinate
dilemma	invalidate	protagonist
disseminate	inveterate	punctilious
divulge	levity	punitive
elucidate	litigation	pusillanimous
endemic	macabre	recapitulation
entrepreneur	malefactor	retract
épée	mandate	retribution
ephemeral	matriarchy	rigour
equitable	mercenary	sanctimonious
equivocal	misanthropist	sinecure
eradicate	monomania	spasmodic
erudite	monopoly	sycophant
euphemism	nullify	symmetry
extemporize	ominous	symposium
facsimile	onus	taciturn
hedonism	ostracize	temerity
heterogeneous	panacea	tremulous
hypochondria	paradox	unilateral
idiosyncrasy	patriarch	verify
implicit	peripatetic	vindicate
impunity	perjury	zenith

2. By using each word in a separate sentence, show the difference in meaning between the words in the following pairs:

advise; inform
affect; effect (as verbs)
allude; mention
appraise; appreciate
aught; ought
balance; surplus
bereft; bereaved
compliment; complement
consigned; assigned
contemptuous; contemptible
continual; continuous

courage; heroism
credible; creditable
deduce; deduct
defective; deficient
deprecate; depreciate
discover; invent
dubious; doubtful
economic; economical
edible; eatable
epitaph; epigram
equable; equitable

facility; faculty
fate; providence
forgone; foregone
formerly; formally
heredity; environment
illegible; unreadable
illicit; elicit
incredulous; incredible
infer; imply
innocuous; innocent
insolvent; insoluble
in to; into
irascible; irate
luxurious; luxuriant
mistake; fault
momentous; momentary
nightly; nocturnal
notable; notorious
past; passed
picturesque; pictorial

practice; practise
principal; principle
proscribe; prescribe
pungent; poignant
reason; excuse
salubrious; salutary
satire; sarcasm
sentiment; sentimentality
stimulate; simulate
stimulus; stimulant
superficial; superfluous
suspicious; suspected
tradition; convention
treason; treachery
uneatable; inedible
uninterested; disinterested
unsatisfied; dissatisfied
valuable; invaluable
venal; venial
voracity; veracity

3. Write brief definitions for the following words to show the basic difference of meaning of each word within the group.

Nouns
(1) solicitor; barrister; magistrate; advocate.
(2) symphony; concerto; sonata; cantata; opera; overture.
(3) novel; romance; satire; epic; elegy; ode; anecdote.
(4) collection; hoard; store; congregation.
(5) news; information; report; data.
(6) perjury; larceny; arson; forgery.
(7) investigation; research; inquest; scrutiny.
(8) journey; excursion; expedition; tour.
(9) pride; arrogance; conceit; vanity.
(10) salary; wages; fee; remuneration.

Adjectives
(11) old; obsolete; venerable; archaic.
(12) durable; lasting; permanent.
(13) original; genuine; authentic.
(14) important; essential; paramount; predominant.
(15) famous; notorious; celebrated; renowned.

Verbs
(16) repair; restore; renovate; rehabilitate; renew; revise.
(17) leave; forsake; withdraw; relinquish.
(18) rival; surpass; emulate; eclipse.
(19) admit; confess; apologize; recant.
(20) erase; expunge; eliminate; obliterate.

4. (1) Write a brief dictionary definition for each of the following words:
a book; a box; a brick; a bus; a cigarette; a clock; a door; a fountain-pen; a house; a kettle; a knife; a policeman; a road; a sailor; a school; a shoe; a soldier; a tree; a typewriter; a window.

(2) Write a synonym for each of the following words:
aggressive; amiable; ancient; assemble; candid; conceal; criterion; emulate; genuine; indict; menacing; minimum; polite; puny; repay; reticent; robust; spurious; stupid; wild.

(3) Write an antonym for each of the following words:
accelerate; affable; ancient; assemble; bright; cleanse; complex; flexible; frail; futile; harmony; imaginary; minimum; misery; miserly; pompous; progressive; reveal; transparent; wild.

(4) For each of the following groups, write a paragraph to include all four words in any order but without altering them in any way.
(a) policy; elevate; practise; stage.
(b) congregate; apologies; innate; plane.
(c) fare; suddenly; electric; pretence.
(d) entertain; stop; agreement; ancient.
(e) peace; trail; treatment; feature.
(f) stamp; intrinsic; habit; costly.
(g) spare; contemporary; order; steam.
(h) course; picture; coast; element.
(i) comment; point; essential; coach.
(j) long; separate; stern; choice.

5. Rewrite the following definitions, explaining all abbreviations in full.
(1) rot, n. & int.   1. Decay (esp. in timber cf. Dry ...)
                     2. (sl.) Nonsense.
[prob. f. Scand. (Icel. Norw. *rot*)]

11

(2) sceptic (sk-), *sk-, n. Person who doubts, (pop.) atheist. So ... ism. n.
[ult. f. Gk. *skeptikos* (prec. . . . ic)]
(3) leal, a. (Sc. & literary). Loyal, honest.
[f. OF *leel* (cf. Loyal) f. L *legalis*, lawful]
(4) schedule (‖sh-), n., & v.t. 1. Tabulated statement of details.
[ME & OF *cedule* f. LL *scedula*]
(5) schism (sizm) n. Division of community into factions.
[f. OF *scisme* f. eccl. L f. Gk *skhisma*—split]
(6) ear^2, n. Spike, head of corn.
[OE *ear* (cf. G. *ahre*, Du. *aar*), cogn. w. L *acus*. husk.]
(7) aught (awt), n. & adv. Anything; (adv., arch.) in any degree or respect.
[OE *awiht* (*a* ever + *wiht* wight); later OE *aht*, gives mod. *ought*, now less usu. form]
(8) jar^2, v.i. & t. (-rr-). Sound discordantly.
[prob. imit.]

6. Replace each of the following phrases by a single word of exactly the same meaning.

(1) A programme of business to be dealt with at a meeting.
(2) The loss in value of machinery through wear and tear.
(3) The identification of a disease by its symptoms.
(4) A state of being forgotten.
(5) To sign one's name on the back of a cheque.
(6) An official numbering of the population.
(7) A period of ten years.
(8) 480 sheets of paper.
(9) A gift under a will.
(10) Not bearing upon the matter in hand.
(11) 24 sheets of paper.
(12) A limited allowance of some commodity.
(13) The same in every respect.
(14) The scientific study of man as an animal.
(15) Divert money fraudulently to one's own use.
(16) An official inspection of accounts.
(17) A situation presenting the choice of two alternatives, both unfavourable.
(18) An exact copy.
(19) A study of antiquities.

(20) One who believes that nothing can be known about the existence of God.
(21) Compulsory enlistment for military service.
(22) A person bearing blame due to others.
(23) Possessing infinite knowledge.
(24) Musical composition for a solo instrument or instruments accompanied by an orchestra.
(25) Time of the year when day and night are the same length.
(26) Having a back-bone.
(27) Remove persons from a place of danger.
(28) Musical instrument comprising wooden bars which are struck by hammers.
(29) Part taken as an example of a whole.
(30) Bring back to life.
(31) The dissection of, or experimenting on, living animals.
(32) Written statement given under oath to be used as judicial evidence.
(33) Based on observation and experiment, not theory.
(34) The act of making unexpected discoveries by accident.
(35) To apply oil as ceremonial baptism or consecration.
(36) Set of contributions on a common subject from various authors and points of view.
(37) Treatment of light and shade in painting.
(38) Government of the state by a select few.
(39) A loan from a building society for the purpose of buying property.
(40) One who suffers punishment for adherence to beliefs.

2. Using language effectively

The importance of grammatical accuracy

We have seen how important it is to use words accurately and effectively. It is equally important to be certain that what we say and write is grammatically correct. Only in this way can we ensure that our readers and listeners understand precisely what we mean. Grammatical faults and ambiguous statements can create serious errors in business which may result in considerable loss of both time and money. It is also discourteous towards other people if we are careless in the way we express ourselves. We must, therefore, pay particular attention to everything we write and say.

The sentence

Since effective expression is achieved only through the medium of the sentence, we must begin with a consideration of the sentence.

A sentence is the statement of a complete thought. It must contain a subject, either stated or understood, and a verb. In casual conversation we may use disjointed phrases, but in all writing and formal speaking, every sentence we use must have a subject and a verb. An example of an incomplete sentence is sometimes found in the opening of a letter.

In reply to your letter of July 6th.

The full stop after '6th' is incorrect since the sentence has no subject and no verb, and is, therefore, not finished. There is a need to indicate who is writing and what the reply is.

In reply to your letter of July 6th, I am writing to inform you that your order has been sent today.

Similarly, 'Thanking you for your assistance', at the end of a letter is also an incomplete sentence, since there is no indication of who is expressing thanks. A correct version would be:

I thank you for your assistance.

In certain examination questions which require the correction of sentences, you will be asked not only to rewrite the sentences but also to explain the mistakes. Although it may be possible to rewrite each sentence avoiding the error by instinct, an identification of the kind of mistake is also necessary.

Common grammatical errors

Non-agreement of subject and verb

We have already established that a sentence must have a subject and a verb. It is also important that these should agree. For example, a singular subject must have a singular verb, a plural subject, a plural verb.

Each of the engineers is to be given details of the new processes.

The details of the new processes are to be given to each engineer.

The error of a singular subject and a plural verb, or vice versa, usually arises when the subject and verb are separated by a number of other words. Remember also that 'each', 'every', 'everyone', 'either', 'neither', 'none' are all singular words.

Most collective nouns are singular, but if the constituent members of the collective noun act as individuals, the verb has to be in the plural.

The jury was able to reach a decision in less than an hour.

BUT

The jury were in disagreement amongst themselves over the verdict.

Similarly demonstrative adjectives and relative pronouns must agree with the words to which they belong.

We cannot afford to buy these type of electric fittings for the factory.

In this case, while creating a grammatical error, the writer has also confused the reader. Is there only one type of fitting being considered or are there a number of them? This sentence can therefore mean:

We cannot afford to buy this type of electric fitting for the factory.
OR
We cannot afford to buy these types of electric fitting for the factory.

Make certain that demonstrative adjectives ('this', 'that', 'these', 'those') agree with the nouns to which they belong.

One further example of the singular-plural confusion is seen in the sentence below.

She is one of the students who is taking the examination.

The relative pronoun 'who' refers not to 'she', but to 'students' since the students are those taking the examination. Therefore, the verb should be plural, 'are', to agree with 'students'.

Subject–object confusion

In the same way that singular and plural words are confused, subject and object cases are sometimes wrongly transposed without the error becoming obvious to the ear.

The hotel had no room available for my wife and I.

Here the phrase 'my wife and I' is the object of the sentence. This can be more clearly seen by omitting the words 'my wife and', so that the sentence is more obviously incorrect.

The hotel had no room available for I.

The correct version of the original sentence is:

The hotel had no room available for my wife and me.

When two persons or things are compared using the words 'than' or 'as', they are in the same case; that is, they are both subject or both object.
Therefore:

He is much happier than *me* in working for the local authority,
should be:

He is much happier than I in working for the local authority.

16

Many people confess that they are not certain of the difference in usage between the relative pronouns 'who' and 'whom'. If you are not sure, there is a simple test which you can apply.
(a) 'who' is the subject and is equivalent to 'he' or 'they'.
(b) 'whom' is the object and represents 'him' or 'them'.
The case of a relative pronoun depends upon its function in the part of the sentence to which it belongs. As a means of checking, isolate the clause in which the relative pronoun appears and make it a separate sentence by replacing the relative pronoun with the appropriate pronoun: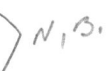

He is the man whom we hope will contribute generously to our funds.

If we separate the clause as suggested above, the result is as follows:

Him will contribute generously to our funds.

This is proof that the relative pronoun in the original sentence should have been 'who'.

Misrelated participle

The misrelated participle is one of the commonest errors which can lead to considerable misunderstanding or absurdity.

Looking at it in daylight, the task appeared easier than expected.

Since the participle is an adjective, the participle phrase 'Looking at it in daylight' should belong to the subject of the sentence, but it is nonsense to suppose that the task was 'looking at it in daylight'. As the sentence stands, there is no indication of who is 'looking'. In addition, we cannot be sure that 'it' refers to 'task'.

The sentence can be corrected in two ways. Either the participle phrase must be replaced, or the subject of the sentence must be changed to make the participle relate to the subject.

Correct versions:

(a) *When he looked at it in daylight, the task appeared easier than expected.*

(b) *Looking at it in daylight, he saw that the task was easier than had been expected.*

Gerund

We objected to him altering the notices.

In the above sentence, the word 'altering' is part of a verb used as a noun (gerund), not a present participle (adjective). We object to the alteration of the notices, not to *him*, so that as a noun, 'altering' must be qualified by an adjective 'his', not a pronoun, 'him'. The sentence could have been written:

We objected to his alteration of the notices.

Thus the error would not have arisen, but there is a slight alteration in the meaning.

Correlatives

Correlative conjunctions go together in pairs as shown below. It is wrong to mix these as usage has dictated they should be arranged in this order.

either .... or
neither .... nor
both .... and
not only .... but also
rather .... than

The first correlative must be placed immediately before the first alternative, and the second before the second alternative.

She is going neither to her son nor to her daughter for Christmas.

Inconsistent use of pronouns

One should always abide by the Highway Code even if it causes him to be late at his destination.

In the sentence above, by using both 'one' and 'he', the writer has implied that two different people are involved. In order to avoid such a confusion, the same pronoun must be maintained throughout. Thus the sentence can be correctly rewritten in two ways:

(a) *One should always abide by the Highway Code even if it causes one to be late at one's destination.*

(b) *He should always abide by the Highway Code even if it causes him to be late at his destination.*

Comparative and superlative confusion

The comparative form of an adjective which usually ends in '-er', or is preceded by 'more', should be used when two items are compared. When three or more items are compared, the superlative form must be used. The superlative form of an adjective usually ends with '-est', or is preceded by 'most'.

John was the younger of the two brothers.
This is the most reliable book there is on the subject.

Shall—will

It is wrong to assume that 'shall' and 'will' are interchangeable without an alteration of meaning.

(a) In a simple statement using the future tense,
'I' and 'we' are followed by 'shall',
'you', 'he', 'she', 'it', 'they' are followed by 'will'.

I shall be taking my driving test next week.

(b) If the writer wishes to convey strong determination in the future, the above rule is reversed.

I will pass my driving test, even if I have to take it a dozen times.

In this way the emphasis of the word 'will' conveys a different meaning from the word 'shall'.

(c) When the writer wishes to express a conditional dependence of one action upon another, he may use the rule (a) above. This suggests a result which is definite or likely to happen.

The alternative 'I/we should', 'he/she/it/they would' introduces an element of doubt. This version is used also when requesting a favour.

I shall . . . . if you will . . .
I should . . . . if you would (could) . . .

The table below may be found useful for reference.

(a) Simple future tense

    I, we } shall   you, he, she, it, they } will

(b) Determination

    I, we } will   you, he, she, it, they } shall

(c) Conditional

I	shall	you	will
		he	
		she	
we	should	it	would
		they	

N.B. All tenses take 'should' when it means 'ought to'.

At Christmas we should think of those less fortunate than ourselves.

'Due to' and 'like'

According to the dictionary, the word 'due' is an adjective and therefore it qualifies a noun or pronoun which usually precedes it in the sentence:

The next train is due to arrive at platform 9.

In this sentence 'due' as an adjective qualifies the subject 'next train'.

'Due' should not be used with 'to' to form a compound preposition. If the phrase 'due to' means 'owing to' or 'because of', it has been incorrectly used and must be replaced by either of these alternatives:

Owing to an increased Bank Rate, it is difficult to obtain home loans.

If you are in doubt, it is better to avoid the phrase 'due to' by revising the wording of the sentence.

Similarly 'like' is an adjective and must not be used as a conjunction in place of 'as':

We are hoping to increase our sales this year as we have done in the past.

Split infinitive

It is necessary to strictly observe the rules of the game.

A split infinitive occurs when a word (usually an adverb) is placed between 'to' and the verb of the infinitive. This is not so much a grammatical error as a clumsy expression and should, therefore, be avoided.

It is necessary to observe strictly the rules of the game.

Ambiguous sentences

Ambiguities of expression arise when a writer chooses or arranges his words carelessly so that a second and unintentional meaning can be derived.

It is easy to imagine the confusion that can arise in any business if people express themselves so badly that what they say or write can be interpreted in more than one way. It is of the utmost importance that we examine all our communications to be certain that what we intend our readers to understand is in no way liable to misinterpretation.

Most ambiguities can be placed in the following classes:

Faulty word order (*The rule of proximity*)

Unfurnished accommodation required by young professional man, about to be married for one year or more.

This is the commonest of errors. Qualifying words and phrases must be placed close to the words to which they belong. A carelessly misplaced word may be in such a position that it belongs to the wrong phrase. Here the phrase 'for one year or more' applies to 'required' not to 'to be married'.

Unfurnished accommodation required for one year or more by young professional man about to be married.

Here the ambiguity was amusing, but in another situation, such an error could be disastrous.

All relative pronouns must clearly refer to the appropriate antecedents.

The word 'only' is often placed arbitrarily in a sentence so that it can apply to more than one word.

I only think that this plan will succeed.

In this sentence, 'only' can qualify both 'I' and 'think'. It should be moved so that it applies to either 'I' or 'think', but not both:

Only I think that this plan will succeed.
I think only that this plan will succeed.

Words of double meaning

The second cause of ambiguity arises when a writer uses a word or phrase which itself has two meanings.

The victims of the earthquake were forced to leave their houses through the cracks which appeared in the walls.

The word 'through' can be interpreted as 'by way of' or 'because of'. Either version is plausible in this instance.

Omission of necessary words

Sometimes, in haste, a writer or speaker will compress his statement so that essential words are omitted.

The judge said the witness was biased.

To make it clear that the judge accused the witness, and not the witness accused the judge, 'that' must be inserted into the sentence.

The judge said that the witness was biased.

Confusion of pronouns

He said his father died when he was young.

If spoken, this sentence can perhaps be made explicit to the listener by the emphasis of the voice, but when written, it is certainly ambiguous.

The clause 'when he was young' can describe the speaker or his father. It is necessary to rephrase the sentence so that it is clear that either the speaker was young, or the father was young.

He said that when he was young, his father had died.

OR

He said that his father had died young.

When asked to rewrite a sentence avoiding any ambiguities, it is advisable to interpret the more plausible meaning, which is usually the one intended by the writer. Often, however, as can be seen above, either meaning is likely, in which case it does not matter which version is written down.

EXERCISES

1. The following sentences contain grammatical errors. Rewrite each sentence correctly and explain your reason for making the corrections.
    (1) I am grateful for all the help you have given my brother and I.
    (2) We have not won nor failed entirely.
    (3) The police wish to interview a man whom they think can help them in their enquiries.
    (4) You could arrange your work neater if you tried.

(5) There were less people in the cinema than they had expected.
(6) They were very pleased to hear of him leaving.
(7) None of those who had been chosen for the team were able to play in the important game.
(8) Due to the fog, many buses were late this morning.
(9) The lecturer could not solve the problem any better than us.
(10) Neither the doctor or the nurse were able to give as much help to the injured man as me.
(11) Reaching the end of the journey, a warm fire greeted the travellers.
(12) He cannot work as quick as me.
(13) Of the two examinations, the candidates were advised to enter for the easiest one.
(14) The soldiers decided to suddenly attack the military railway bridge.
(15) This is one of the plays which was recommended by the newspaper critic.
(16) They were very annoyed at him failing his driving test.
(17) I am writing to inform you that having been placed on the short-list, the Selection Board will interview you on Friday next at 10.45 a.m.
(18) In reply to your letter of 6th April regarding an order for six tons of boiler fuel.
(19) When the Chairman opened the meeting, there was seen in the hall many people who could not find vacant seats.
(20) The 'Mona Lisa' with other paintings from the Louvre were sent on loan to the United States.
(21) He is the only man who you can trust.
(22) Thinking about the coming examination, his chance of passing seemed slight.
(23) I never remember him telling me of his success.
(24) If it was possible to guess the outcome of the next election, we would save ourselves much trouble.
(25) Neither of the rooms were really comfortable.
(26) It was reported that many people had died in India due to the famine.
(27) There was no reason why the train should not be late as it was on time at the previous station.
(28) The police were not only concerned with finding the criminal but proving his guilt.
(29) He is one of the cricketers whom we hope is going to score many runs this season.

(30) No sooner had we started out when it began to rain.
(31) The crowd was undecided whether to go home or wait in the rain.
(32) I wrote to ask my brother if he would give me his collection of books and would he let me have the bookshelves as well?
(33) I shall be most grateful if you would send me a copy of your gramophone record catalogue.
(34) At the concert, the orchestral players watched the conductor like they had been told to do.
(35) I could not help but overhear you asking the way to the Post Office.

2. Rewrite the following sentences removing any ambiguities or absurdities which have arisen.
 (1) Erected in memory of F. Jones drowned in the River Thames by his fellow directors.
 (2) Only the girls who had passed the entrance test were allowed to continue the course.
 (3) The cost of the books was ten shillings more than the schoolboy expected.
 (4) I have lost no time in reading this book.
 (5) A knock came at the door. It was the parcel of books.
 (6) We only hope that all will be well.
 (7) The vicar said he would wear no clothes to distinguish him from his parishioners.
 (8) Everyone agreed with the choice of the chairman.
 (9) He did not die happily.
 (10) Notice on Southend Pier: Do not throw people underneath.
 (11) No one he knew could solve the problem.
 (12) He did not wish to see me particularly.
 (13) The manager reserves the right to exclude those whom he thinks proper.
 (14) Advertisement in the *Monumental Journal*: Carver seeks permanent position in marble and stone.
 (15) Those who have relatives buried in this cemetery are requested to keep them in order.
 (16) The enemy soldiers were a constant threat and one went about at night armed with a gun.
 (17) Chemist's advertisement: We dispense with accuracy.
 (18) I did not know the Director said the Secretary was arranging the meeting.

(19) Outside the shop he met Mary and her cousin Jane joined them inside the building.
(20) The landlord told his tenant that he would have to move to a larger house.
(21) He explained to them all the difficulties.
(22) Most of our roads today need badly improving.
(23) When did you ask me to phone you?
(24) I nearly saw a man run over last week.
(25) Donations towards the cost of the Old People's Home should be sent to the above address which will be gratefully received.
(26) Mr. Wolf told Mr. Bax that his son had won the first prize.
(27) One can only consider a holiday on the continent if one has enough money to pay for it.
(28) The convict was seen at once by the policeman running across the bridge.
(29) We must not take an unwise decision until we have all the information before us.
(30) The measures taken have only been partially successful.
(31) Girls can become engineers as well as boys.
(32) It was very hot in Barcelona which we did not like.
(33) 'Our meat comes directly from local farmers killed on the premises.'
(34) When did you ask me to write to you?
(35) A line of people stretched down the corridor which was getting longer every minute.

3. The mechanics of style

Why punctuate?

The purpose of punctuation is to make whatever is written easier to understand and to render, as closely as possible, the spoken emphasis of the words. Its importance in written communication is considerable since misunderstandings can easily arise from faulty punctuation. The so-called 'rules' of punctuation are really the established forms which have been created through usage.

The rules of punctuation

A full stop is used:
- (a) at the end of a sentence.
- (b) after abbreviations:

    e.g., *M.A.*, *C.O.D.*

If the first and last letter of the abbreviation are the same as those of the word, the full stop is often omitted:

    Mr Dr St (*saint*)

A comma is used:

(a) to mark a short pause in a sentence in order to make the emphasis and meaning clear:

The journey was six miles, longer than we had expected.

(b) before a subordinate clause:

James Fleming was awarded the Victoria Cross, but he died before receiving the medal.

(c) before and after qualifying words and phrases:

It was hoped that the Festival, the first of its kind, would be a great success.

(d) before and after words in apposition:

Mr. Sandford, the Secretary, was elected for a second year in office.

(e) before 'and' where 'and' begins a separate clause:

The rain had fallen all morning, and it was not expected to stop before the opening of the match.

(f) between separate items in a list or series:

*Ships, towers, domes, theatres and temples lie,
Open unto the fields, and to the sky.*

(*Wordsworth*)

(g) to separate direct and indirect speech in the same sentence:

Mr. Teal opened the book and said, 'I will offer you twenty pence for this.'

(h) to separate names in address:

I think you should speak to me, Mr. Dubarry.

N.B. Remember that too many commas in a sentence will cause as much confusion to the reader as too few.

A question mark is used after all direct questions:

Where can you find such a quiet place in the whole of England?

A question mark acts in place of either a comma or a full stop.
An indirect question does not take a question mark:

I wonder where you can find such a quiet place in the whole of England.

A supposition does not take a question mark:

I suppose you will require a day's holiday as compensation for the overtime you have worked.

An exclamation mark is used after an interjection or an exclamatory sentence:

'It's wonderful!' he said.
'Help!' she cried.

Exclamation marks are rare; they should be used only when something is said in surprise, or for particular emphasis.

A semicolon is used:

(a) between two statements which are themselves separate sentences but are so closely linked and balanced that a full stop would constitute too strong a break.

Again I had no luck; I could not find the book I wanted.

(b) between two clauses which are balanced, but require a more definite separation than would arise with a comma:

Seeing her opportunity, Mrs. Norman walked away into the house; and Fanny found herself alone with Mr. Crawford.

(Jane Austen)

A colon is used before a quotation, examples, or lists of items:

There are three qualities which every athlete should possess: fitness, quickness of mind, and perseverance.

A hyphen is used:

(a) to join two words considered as an entity, or between a prefix and the main word in order to clarify the meaning or pronunciation:

anti-aircraft, co-operative, pro-nationalist,

(b) to link compound words:

south-east, court-martial, owner-occupier, brother-in-law.

A dash is used:

(a) to indicate an interruption or interpolation:

'Do you think I might—'
'No,' he replied.

(b) to give emphasis:

'What can they—dare they—do to me?'

(c) to denote hesitation in direct speech, or pauses in time during conversation:

'I am sure you must be—yes—so you don't know me—I could have sworn—why it is my old friend Jack.'

Inverted commas are used to indicate:
   (a) direct speech:
'*Don't think we shall surrender without a fight,*' *shouted the Colonel. The Captain replied,* '*You will have only yourself to blame for the consequences.*'

Note: (i) that a separate paragraph is required for the words of each speaker; (ii) that a capital letter is used to open the actual words quoted.

   (b) direct quotations:

A quotation within direct speech is indicated by double inverted commas within the single inverted commas or vice versa.

'*I saw only one notice which said "No Parking",*' *explained the accused.*

   (c) slang or words used sarcastically:

'*punch-up*', *so-called* '*experts*'.

   (d) Titles of books, ships, newspapers, houses, trade names, etc.:

'*The Times*', '*Queen Mary*', '*Hamlet*'.

The apostrophe is used:
   (a) to indicate possession:
singular form before the 's':

the boy's cap.

plural form after the 's':

the boys' shoes.

Words whose plural form does not take an 's', have the apostrophe before the added 's':

men's, children's.

Names ending in 's' in the singular form often do not take an additional 's' in the possessive form:

Brahms' Symphonies, St. James' Street.
This avoids the need to pronounce the 's' sound three times in succession.

   (b) to indicate missing letters:

I'm, don't, o'clock.

   (c) to indicate plural forms of figures:
10's, 1920's.

No apostrophe is used in yours, theirs, ours, its, hers. *But, N.B.* one's.

Recording the spoken word

Direct speech is a record of the exact words spoken. If this is in the form of a dialogue, the words quoted are placed in inverted commas:

'*You will have to write this piece again,*' *said the editor.*
'*There will hardly be enough time,*' *remarked the reporter.*

When the passage is presented in dramatic form, the names of the speakers appear in the margin, and the inverted commas are omitted:

Editor: *You will have to write this piece again.*
Reporter: *There will hardly be enough time.*

In both cases, a separate paragraph is used for the words of each speaker.

Indirect or reported speech is an account of what the speaker said as presented by someone else. Since this account must be of speech which had taken place earlier, the tenses of the verbs are changed from the present to the past. In addition, as reported speech is not a quotation, inverted commas are omitted:

The editor told the reporter that he would have to write the piece again, to which the reporter replied that there would hardly be enough time.

Reported speech is frequently used in business. In the writing of reports, all first-hand evidence collected verbatim is presented in the form of reported speech, unless a direct quotation from a particular source is necessary.

Similarly, the minutes of a meeting are always written in reported speech. The secretary makes notes of the proceedings, but does not take down a record of the actual words spoken. For this reason, the minutes, when written up later, are an abbreviated account of the important transactions of the meeting presented as reported speech.

Rules for changing direct speech to reported speech

Pronouns and possessive adjectives

The first and second person of the direct speech become third person in reported speech.

Direct	*Reported*
I	he: she
we	they

me	him: her
us	them
you (subject)	he: she: they
you (object)	him: her: them
my	his: her
our	their
your	their

Tenses

In reported speech present tenses become past: future becomes future in the past.

Direct	Reported
shall	should
will	would
may	might
can	could
has: have	had

Verbs already in the past tense in the direct speech become past perfect tense in the reported speech:

Direct: '*I went to Paris for my holiday,*' he said.

Reported: *He said that he had been to Paris for his holiday.*

N.B. If the direct speech passage concerns an ever-present factor, the verbs must be retained as present tense in the reported speech:

Direct: '*The flowers in Greece at springtime are a wonderful sight,*' said the guide.

Reported: *The guide said that the flowers in Greece at springtime are a wonderful sight.*

Time and place changes

Direct	Reported
now	then
here	there
yesterday	the previous day
today	that day
tomorrow	the following day

Direct questions and commands

Direct questions and commands become indirect questions and commands:

Direct: *'Will you be using this room tonight?'* asked the secretary.

Reported: The secretary asked whether he would be using the room that evening.

Direct: *'Go to bed,'* said his mother.

Reported: His mother ordered him to go to bed.

Introductory phrases

All polite introductions—'Ladies and Gentlemen', 'Mr. Chairman'—are omitted in reported speech.

Hints on reporting speech

(a) Avoid the unnecessary use of the names of the speakers, but beware of the ambiguous 'he', 'him', 'they', 'them' which easily arise if the original dialogue is between two people of the same sex.

(b) Use more meaningful words than 'tell', 'ask', and 'say', to give a clearer indication of the manner in which something was said. Verbs such as 'urged', 'complained', 'repeated', 'suggested', 'appealed', 'threatened', etc., will obviate the necessity for additional adverbs and adverbial phrases.

(c) Keep the total number of words in the reported version as low as possible. So often passages of reported speech become clumsy and verbose.

(d) In dialogue, sentences are often very short. Try to join together into one sentence the speech of more than one speaker. If possible include question and answer in the same sentence.

Direct: *Aunt: Where have you been?*
David: I will not tell you.

Reported: When his aunt asked him where he had been, David refused to tell her.

This provides greater continuity and overcomes the turgidity of style which is often found in reported speech.

(e) At the end of the exercise, read both the original and the reported version to see that every phrase and implication has been included. Carefully scrutinize the reported speech to be sure that it is idiomatic English which avoids repetition and pomposity.

EXERCISES

Punctuate the following passages.

1. Of late years an abundant shower of curates has fallen upon the north of England. They lie very thick on the hills; every parish has one or more of them; they are young enough to be very active, and ought to be doing a great deal of good. If you think from this prelude that anything like a romance is preparing for you, readers, you never were more mistaken. Do you anticipate sentiment and poetry and reveries? Do you expect passion, stimulus, and melodrama? Calm your expectations; reduce them to a lowly standard. Something real, cool, and solid lies before you; something unromantic as Monday morning, when all who have work wake with the consciousness that they must rise and betake themselves thereto.
Shirley, Charlotte Brontë.

2. The Moslem quarter of a city is lonely and desolate. You go up and down, and on over shelving and hillocky paths through the narrow lanes walled in by blank windowless dwellings. You come out upon an open space strewed with the black ruins that some late fire has left. You pass by a mountain of castaway things, the rubbish of centuries, and on it you see numbers of big wolf-like dogs lying torpid under the sun, with limbs outstretched to the full, as if they were dead. Storks or cranes, sitting fearless upon the low roofs, look gravely down upon you.
Eothen, A. W. Kingslake.

3. Aminta received a case from one of the footmen. "What is that, my dear?" said Mrs Pagnell. Aminta unlocked and laid it open. A pair of pistols met Mrs Pagnell's gaze. "We shan't be in need of those things," she said. "One never knows on the road, aunt," replied Aminta. "Pistols!" exclaimed Mrs Pagnell. "One would fancy you think we are in the middle of the last century."
Lord Ormont and his Aminta, George Meredith.

4. "What day is this?" he asked of the waiter, who was making preparations for his dinner. "Day, sir? Is it Wednesday?" "Wednesday, sir? No, sir. Thursday, sir." "I forgot. How goes the time? My watch is unwound." "A few minutes before five o'clock, sir. Been travelling a long time, sir, perhaps?" "Yes." "By rail, sir?" "Yes." "Very confusing, sir. Not much in the habit of travelling by rail myself, sir, but gentlemen frequently say so." "Do many gentlemen come here?" "Pretty well, sir, in general."
Dombey and Son, Charles Dickens.

33

5. officer said mr fang whats this fellow charged with hes not charged at all your worship replied the officer he appears against the boy your worship his worship knew this perfectly well but it was a good annoyance and a safe one appears against the boy does he said fang surveying mr brownlow contemptuously from head to foot swear him before i am sworn i must beg to say one word said mr brownlow and that is that i really never without actual experience could have believed hold your tongue sir said mr fang peremptorily i will not sir replied the old gentleman

Oliver Twist, Charles Dickens.

6. spare no money i said to roscoe let everything on the snark be of the best and never mind decoration plain pine boards is good enough finishing for me but put the money into the construction let the snark be as staunch and strong as any boat afloat never mind what it costs to make her staunch and strong you see that she is made staunch and strong and ill go on writing and earn the money to pay for it and i did as well as i could for the snark ate up money faster than i could earn it

The Cruise of the Snark, Jack London.

7. master marner he said in a conciliatory tone whats lacking to you whats your business here robbed said silas gaspingly ive been robbed i want the constable and the justice and squire cass and mr crackenthorp lay hold on him jem rodney said the landlord hes off his head i doubt hes wet through come and lay hold on him yourself mr snell if youve a mind said jem sullenly hes been robbed and murdered too for what i know he added in a muttering tone

Silas Marner, George Eliot.

8. (a) applications are invited for the appointment of state enrolled nurses non resident for work in wards and out patients departments and for escort duties whitley scales and conditions apply matron st thomas hospital london s e 1

(b) clerical staff male or female single ages 15 30 required attractive salary scales ranging from £220 p a at age 15 to £520 p a male £480 p a female apply in writing stating age experience etc to personnel officer hearts of oak benefit society euston road london n w 1

Royal Society of Arts.

9. morning mr snooks please place twenty pounds of this cheque to my wifes deposit account and forty pounds to my daughters current account certainly mr smith how is pamela enjoying life at cambridge it seems only yesterday she won the lady purses trophy in the junior section of the pony club and now she is an undergraduate oh enjoying herself immensely good by the way the manager would like to talk to you about your insurance with the self security company is he free now yes and hed be pleased to see you
Institute of Bankers.

10. a merry christmas uncle god save you cried a cheerful voice it was the voice of scrooges nephew who came upon him so quickly that this was the first intimation he had of his approach bah said scrooge humbug he had so heated himself with rapid walking in the fog and frost this nephew of scrooges that he was all in a glow his face was ruddy and handsome his eyes sparkled and his breath smoked again christmas a humbug uncle said scrooges nephew you dont mean that im sure i do said scrooge merry christmas what right have you to be merry youre poor enough come then returned the nephew gaily what right have you to be dismal youre rich enough
A Christmas Carol, Charles Dickens.

11. Rewrite the following passage in direct speech, taking dramatic form, with the names of the speaker in the margin.

Mr. Drake asked how long he would be kept waiting. He had given clear instructions the previous day that there was to be no delay. The chief clerk objected firmly but politely that he had received no instructions and that he was fully occupied with the day's schedule and could not ... Mr. Drake broke in with an exclamation. His instructions could not have been understood. He ordered the chief clerk to get on with the invoice at once.
Royal Society of Arts.

12. Rewrite the following passage in direct speech. Begin: The Chairman said, ' ...

The Chairman said that their profits for the year ending September 19— had declined, but it was hoped that the improved export figures would soon compensate for losses at home.

The Board were recommending a dividend of 12% which would signify their confidence in the future.

The previous year he had made reference to the overseas subsidiaries. He was pleased to be able to report that negotiations were well under way for considerable expansion in this field.

The credit squeeze had been the cause of a drop in sales of some electrical appliances, but they were still one of the leading firms in the industry.

The Board felt that there were attractive prospects ahead of them, and with increased determination, improved results would come in the fields of manufacture and selling.

13. Rewrite the following passage in direct speech, beginning: The Minister of Aviation said, '...

The Minister of Aviation said that the Government fully accepted the case that the aircraft industry in this country required a guarantee that projects already agreed would not be cancelled. The industry was facing determined competition in world markets. He said that he was concerned that this challenge would be met successfully. It was the duty of the Government to support them in this respect, but the industry could save itself by its own exertions. Everything possible ought to be done so that the industry could become self-supporting by the end of the following year.

14. Rewrite the following extract in direct speech, beginning: The Chairman said, '...

The Chairman said that the previous year had not been one without difficulties. Nevertheless the Company's turnover had been maintained at the same level as the year before. The importing of cotton goods from the Far East would continue to create problems for the home industry. In his report for the previous year the Chairman had commented upon the reluctance of the Government to place further restrictions upon imported textiles, but he had no better news to report to those present.

Another problem which had faced them was the cut in the quota of imports into West Africa. Fortunately the firm had already large stock in Nigeria and Ghana, but the restriction might affect profits in the future.

15. Rewrite the following passage in reported speech.

Macheath (to Lucy and Polly): My dear Lucy! My dear Polly! Whatsoever hath passed between us is now at an end. If you are fond of marrying again, the best advice I can give you is to ship yourselves off to the West Indies, where you have a fair chance of getting a husband apiece; or by good luck, two or three, as you like best.

The Beggar's Opera (*1728*), John Gay.

16. Rewrite the following in reported speech:

Counsel: Do you admit, Mr. Smith, that you could have gone to the rescue of the bank messenger when he was first attacked by the accused?

Witness: I can only repeat that my surprise on seeing a masked intruder made any action on my part momentarily impossible.

Counsel: But, surely, you must have been spurred to action when the intruder proceeded to attack your old friend the cashier?

Judge (intervening): I think my learned friend must accept the testimony of the witness. Apparently, surprise, or some other agency, prevented the witness from taking any action to help his friends and colleagues.

Institute of Bankers.

17. Rewrite the following extract in reported speech, beginning: The Chairman stated that . . .

The 133rd Annual General Meeting of the National Provincial Bank Limited will be held on February 17th, 19—, at the Head Office, 15, Bishopsgate, London, E.C.2.

The following is the statement by the Chairman, David John Robarts, Esq.:

'We are wonderfully fortunate in the quality and skill of our staff and in their great spirit of loyalty to the Bank and I take this opportunity of thanking them for their hard and efficient work during the past year. Over the years we have negotiated with our Staff Association and Ladies Guild on matters affecting pay and conditions of service. In this respect 19— was an eventful year; following discussions, we made an offer to our staff based on a general increase of 5 per cent with effect from the 1st April 19—, together with special improvements effective from 1st July, 19—, in the salary scales of the younger staff. This offer was not acceptable to the Staff Association or to the Ladies Guild, who requested arbitration, to which they have a legal right under the agreements we have with them. Arising from this, an award was made on the 22nd October, 19—, the effect of which was to vary only slightly the offer already made by the Bank.

As is well known, the pay settlements reached by the clearing banks in 19— were the subject of investigation by the National Board for Prices and Incomes, who concluded, *inter alia*, that the settlements and, in our case, the arbitration award, could not be justified as exceptional pay increases within the criteria of the White Paper. The Board also recommended that, in order to bring the settlements into line with the White Paper, the clearing banks should make no further general pay increase until early next year.

In the whole conduct of our business we do pay great attention to the national interest. However, it needs to be emphasized that we must have conditions of employment which will attract entrants of the appropriate calibre for the proper conduct of the Bank's affairs and we must feel free to examine from time to time all matters relating to the terms of employment of our staff.

National Provincial Bank.
(*Reprinted by permission*)

18. Rewrite the following passage in reported speech.

'So you've got the kid,' said Sikes.
'Yes, here he is,' replied Nancy.
'Did he come quietly?' inquired Sikes.
'Like a lamb,' rejoined Nancy.
'I'm glad to hear it,' said Sikes, 'for the sake of his carcase: as would otherways have suffered for it. Come here, young un; and let me read you a lectur', which is as well got over at once.'

Oliver Twist (1837), Charles Dickens.

19. Rewrite the following speech in reported speech.

Mr. Styles: I wish to present a warning to the meeting. If we are to continue as a successful organization, we must be prepared to spend money on replacing the old equipment. Unless we do this, I am sure that our production, which at present shows no increase over last year, will gradually fall to such a level that we shall be unable to accept any further orders from new customers.

20. Rewrite the following extract in reported speech.

'Whom have you upstairs in the parlour?' asked Mr. Helstone.
'Oh! Mr. Helstone, is it you sir? I could hardly see you for the darkness; it is so soon dark now. Will you walk in sir?'

'I want to know, first, whether it is worth my while walking in. Whom have you upstairs?'
'The curates, sir.'
'What! All of them!'
'Yes, sir.'
'Been dining here?'
'Yes, sir.'
Shirley (1849), Charlotte Brontë.

21. Rewrite the following extract in reported speech beginning: The Minister of Power, Mr Lee, said that . . .

'It is in the interests of the country and of the gas industry that North Sea gas should be exploited and made available on shore as rapidly as possible. In view of this, I gave assistance and advice to both parties in composing the ultimate differences between them.

As a result of the agreement now concluded, the preparatory work can go forward with all speed so that full use may be made of the summer period this year for operations, including pipe-laying at sea.'

Giving the main features of the arrangements between the Council and B.P., he said: 'The Company undertake to deliver and the Council to accept at least 50 million cubic feet a day for 15 years from the commencement of the supply.

The Company will use their best endeavours to increase output to 100 million cubic feet a day during the first three years of supply, and will offer these additional supplies to the Gas Council, who undertake to receive them on a pre-arranged programme.

The agreement also contemplates the possibility of further increasing the quantity of gas to be delivered up to 200 million cubic feet a day.

British Petroleum will from the outset and at their own risk provide a marine pipe capable of carrying 200 million cubic feet a day and the Gas Council will make at least equivalent provision on land.'

Mr. Lee, Minister of Power.
(Reprinted by permission)

22. Rewrite the following passage in reported speech.
'Person's a waitin',' said Sam.
'Does the person want me, Sam?' inquired Mr. Pickwick.

'He wants you particklar; and no one else'll do,' replied Mr. Weller.

'He. Is it a gentleman?' said Mr. Pickwick.

'A very good imitation o' one, if it an't,' replied Mr. Weller.

'But this is a lady's visiting card,' said Mr. Pickwick.

'Given me by a gen't'm'n, hows'ever,' replied Sam, 'and he's a waitin' in the drawing room.'

The Pickwick Papers (1836), Charles Dickens.

23. Rewrite the following passage in reported speech.

'Mr. Bingley is just what a young man ought to be,' said Jane, 'sensible, good-humoured, lively; and I never saw such good manners.'

'He is also handsome,' replied Elizabeth; 'which a young man ought likewise to be, if he possibly can. His character is thereby complete.'

'I was very much flattered by his asking me to dance a second time. I did not expect such a compliment.'

'Did you not? I did for you. But that is one great difference between us. Compliments always take you by surprise, and me never.'

Pride and Prejudice (1813), Jane Austen.

24. Rewrite the following passage in reported speech.

Chairman: I think we all have a copy of the revised plan. Is there anyone present who has not received one?

Mr. James: I am very sorry, Mr. Chairman. I have carelessly forgotten to bring the one I was sent.

Chairman: The Secretary will let you have another, Mr. James. I should like to hear the views of the Committee on the proposed alteration of the route which the new road will take.

Mr. Franks: I feel that this plan makes so little change we might be better served by the original proposals.

Mr. Hall: No, I disagree. In the new plan we have before us, the road can be built close to the railway without the need to construct an embankment. Don't you think this will save us both time and money?

Chairman: If you wish to compare costs, we shall have to consult the estimates for the first plan. Would you, Mr. Secretary, look up the figures for the cost of the original plan?

25. Rewrite the following passage in reported speech, including the stage directions.

Lady Windermere is at table arranging roses in a blue bowl.
Enter Parker.
Parker: Is your ladyship at home this afternoon?
Lady Windermere: Yes—who has called?
Parker: Lord Darlington, my lady.
Lady Windermere: (hesitates for a moment) Show him up—and I'm at home to any one who calls.
Parker: Yes, my lady. (Exit).
Lady Windermere: It's best for me to see him before to-night. I'm glad he's come.
Enter Parker.
Parker: Lord Darlington.
Enter Lord Darlington.
Exit Parker.
Lord Darlington: How do you do, Lady Windermere?
Lady Windermere: How do you do, Lord Darlington? No, I can't shake hands with you. My hands are all wet with these roses. Aren't they lovely. They came from Selby this morning.
Lord Darlington: They are quite perfect.

Lady Windermere's Fan (1892), Oscar Wilde.

4. Writing essays

The essay as a means of communication

The general essay is intended to give you an opportunity of setting out your own views on a variety of subjects. It is not so much a test of knowledge as an exercise in self-expression and communication. The essay is the most accurate method of assessing your ability to communicate, and for this reason is given a prominent place in almost all English examination papers.

In the modern business world, junior executives are often required to submit ideas regarding the company's policy or methods. They may also need to draft reports on new products or proposals, outlining factors for and against their acceptance, and making a final recommendation in the light of the arguments presented. An ability to communicate clearly and concisely on these matters is of utmost importance.

Practice in essay writing is an excellent way to develop such fluency of expression. For example, the ideas for inclusion in an essay must be collected and arranged in a logical order just as the items for inclusion in a report must be carefully assembled and presented in the correct order. Similarly, the end of the report, like the end of the essay, should reach a definite conclusion as a result of the arguments presented.

The examination essay

The essay constitutes the most important single question in most English examination papers. Remember it is the essay which the examiner usually reads first and thus it gives him his initial impression of your ability.

The essay subjects which are set in the English papers of the professional examining boards require you to think for yourself and express your thoughts in a logical form, developing the arguments and establishing critical judgements on the topics under discussion. The ability to do this is essential for a successful business career.

Choose wisely

The trouble with writing an essay usually starts right at the beginning. All too often the candidate sits, pen poised, gazing blankly at a list of essay titles. *Choose ONE of the following . . .* The problem is—which one?

The potentiality of each essay subject must be carefully estimated before you choose what, at first sight, may appear to be the 'easiest' title. Everyone presumably is qualified to write on the subject of the school he or she attended. However, since most schools have the same basic features of design, routine, and syllabus, it will require skill on your part to make your description different from those of all the other candidates who select this topic. Essays on such unimaginative topics can be inconceivably dull. Remember, your essay must interest the examiner. Therefore, study all the subjects very carefully, and then select the one on which you feel you can write the most interesting essay.

Overseas students

Overseas students have a particular advantage in essay writing. By reference to the customs and way of life in their home country, they can treat the essay in an original manner which makes their work quite different and personal. An examiner will find an increased interest in an essay entitled 'A critical account of my education' if it is a description of schools abroad. The overseas student must make it clear that he is referring to his own country, otherwise the reader may become confused by strange items of information.

Plan carefully

Once you have chosen your subject, don't write a word. Sit and think. Then jot down all the ideas that occur to you which might be included in the essay. From these points establish a plan of paragraphs, linking together similar points and creating a logical sequence of thoughts.

It is unlikely that you will think of every point to be included in the essay during the few minutes of preparation before embarking on the subject, but you must have a clear picture in your mind of the conclusion you intend to reach and the way in which you intend to reach it before committing pen to paper. Choose only those arguments which are relevant to your train of thought, which lead logically to your desired conclusion.

When you are planning your essay, frequently look back at the title to see that you are keeping to the subject exactly as it has been stated. So often candidates forget the precise details of the title and embark on a general essay far beyond the limitations of the given subject. For example, an essay entitled 'The influence of advertising' must not be allowed to develop into a general essay on advertising. The whole purpose of an essay on this topic should be an evaluation of the influence which advertising exerts on the public with specific examples quoted to support your statements.

Use an appropriate style

Do not attempt to write a humorous or satirical essay unless you are convinced that it is the appropriate treatment for the subject. Remember, the examiner may consider your hilarious essay a frivolous waste of time. On the other hand, an element of humour, aptly introduced into an otherwise serious essay, may enliven the text with most beneficial results.

Give specific examples and details to illustrate general statements. The inclusion of a personal account will at once make your essay different from all the others on the same subject. An autobiographical approach to topics should be handled with care and adopted only when the subject requires it. You may have some interesting views on such a subject as 'Road Safety' supported by personal incidents which will suitably illustrate your points. To write such an essay in the first person singular would, however, be a mistake.

Check carefully

At the end of the essay, read through what you have written to correct any errors of grammar or spelling which may have occurred through haste. When the whole paper is completed, read through the essay again; this gives you an opportunity for revisions which may come to mind while you are dealing with the rest of the paper. It is a wise precaution to leave half a page blank at the end of the essay where you can add further material. If necessary, it is possible to write an extra paragraph here, giving clear instructions to the examiner where it should be placed in the body of the essay.

Learn as you go

Keep all the essays that have been marked by your tutor. In this way you will be able to note the errors which you make most frequently; an awareness of these mistakes will help you to avoid them in future essays and in the examination itself. For the same reason, make a note of all spelling errors and learn the correct versions.

It is advisable for all candidates taking examinations in English to read at least one informative newspaper every day including Sunday. Newspapers provide an enormous range of information and opinion on current affairs which may well have a bearing on a number of essay subjects. A high standard of journalism will also provide a suitable model to imitate and will help to broaden your vocabulary.

Essay types

Essay topics can be divided into five groups: (a) Descriptive, (b) Discussion, (c) Narrative, (d) A review of a book, film or play, (e) Character study. Sometimes a letter is offered as an alternative to the more usual essay title.

Descriptive. Essays which fall into this category are always the most popular, but often a subject is chosen as a last resort by those who are afraid to attempt any topic which appears to ask for personal opinions and judgement. 'A village cricket match' presents a wide range of ideas to a writer of imagination with a penetrating eye for detail and humour. Those who choose such a title as a line of least resistance, because it appears to be an easy subject, make the mistake of mentioning only the most obvious factors relating to any cricket match, so that their essays are alike. At a village cricket match, a description of the participants and spectators will be of much greater interest than the game itself.

Discussion. A few essay subjects require a specialist knowledge; you should consider such topics only if you are completely familiar with the facts.

Some candidates feel intimidated by the dogmatic or provocative manner in which some subjects are presented, and are misled into thinking that the wording of the title reflects the examiner's own opinion. 'Blood sports should be abolished', does not suggest that if you disagree with this statement you will be in conflict with the examiner.

Evidence must be quoted to support the case you are presenting. It is a mistake to appear impartial regarding controversial matters. However, all arguments have two sides. You should be able to refute opposing views logically and rationally. If you have no personal opinions on provocative subjects, you are unlikely to write an interesting essay.

Many essay topics may be treated as both description and discussion. The one-word title allows complete freedom in the choice of the character of the essay. 'Roads', for example, can include a history of roads, a description of the different types of road, and a criticism of the roads in this country with suggestions for their improvement.

Narrative. The narrative essay should be avoided by those who have had no experience of writing short stories. Such an essay requires a clear plan of events, presenting episodes in the correct sequence with a climax towards which the opening paragraphs lead. The conclusion of the story must be determined before the first sentence is written. A narrative essay is not intended as an experiment in formless improvisation; any dialogue which is included must have a direct bearing on the story itself.

'A daring rescue' should be predominantly about the rescue itself without a lengthy introduction, and an act of daring ought to be the central incident of the story related.

If you intend to write a narrative essay in the examination, you should read a number of short stories to see how professional authors treat their subjects. In this way you can model your style on that of an experienced writer.

Review. A review of a book, film, or play does not include an account of the plot. Only the barest outline of the story is given in order to establish the situation and identity of the characters. The important part of this essay is the candidate's assessment of the work—the appeal to the reader or audience—its strength and weakness—the manipulation of plot and development of character—comparison with similar works, or ones by the same author. In this way the essay could be classified as a discussion, but not as a description. Specific examples or incidents should be briefly quoted or used as references in support of critical comments so that the reader can himself make some judgement in the light of your remarks, although he had not read the book or seen the play.

Read the reviews of films, books and broadcasts which appear in the Sunday newspapers and on certain days in most of the weekly newspapers. This will enable you to see the manner in which professional critics approach their subjects.

Character study. A character study is basically a descriptive essay of a specific nature. If the essay is primarily about a man's work, his character should emerge from an account of his achievements. This essay must begin with a clear statement of who the man is, giving a very brief personal history if necessary. The bulk of the essay should consist of a critical assessment of the man's personality. The candidate needs to build up a clear picture of the man to bring him to life.

The extended essay

Candidates taking the Ordinary National Diploma or Ordinary National Certificate in Business Studies are required to complete an essay of 3,000–5,000 words on a subject of a commercial, industrial, or professional nature.

Choice of subject

The choice of a subject must be made with care. First select a field of interest and then take a particular aspect of it which can be covered adequately in some detail. 'Advertising', as a topic, presents too wide a scope, and an essay of this kind could be written without resort to any reference matter at all. 'The Advertisers' Code with regard to Commercial Television' limits the field to be covered and will produce an essay of much greater value.

Taking a restricted subject will make the task of finding suitable material in books, magazines, and newspapers a more manageable one. Four or five references to your specialized topic in a book may be of more use to you than a whole book which covers a wider subject.

When you have begun work on your essay, you may find that you have sufficient material to limit your essay to an even narrower aspect of your original subject. Covering a particular theme in detail will always be of greater validity than an introduction to a larger general topic.

Preliminary research

Knowing someone who is connected professionally with the subject on which you are writing your essay may assist you in your search for material. For example, in order to write an essay on life assurance, it would be useful to be acquainted with a person who works for an insurance company who can provide you with up-to-date information and the titles of books which will be of value in your research.

Many business organizations and professional bodies are prepared to assist students by providing booklets and other information which may not otherwise be obtainable. The publicity or public relations department of certain firms will supply pamphlets and other material usually issued to the trade, but not available to the general public. When you write to them you should make your request clearly and courteously, indicating the purpose and scope of your essay and the information you require. Trade magazines often contain articles which may have a bearing upon your essay and will include advertisements from the leading organizations in their field. In this way you can obtain the names and addresses of specialist firms who might be of assistance to you.

At your college or local library ask if you may look through recent back numbers of weekly journals such as *The Economist* and *The Banker* which carry articles on a wide range of subjects of interests to those concerned with business studies. Also look regularly at the business pages in the daily and Sunday newspapers for recent information. Remember that when a book is published, it may already be out of date; although a book can provide a sound basis for your essay, recent facts and statistical data will be found only in current magazines and newspapers.

Draft plan

When you have assembled sufficient material to begin, compile a draft plan of the essay and choose a provisional title. Both these may undergo a change as you progress with the writing, but keep a careful watch on the overall shape of the essay.

Many essays are satisfactorily divided into 'chapters' with subheadings. Prepare a synopsis of the entire essay under sectional headings so that if necessary the parts of the essay can be treated separately.

Wait until the whole work is complete before typing or writing it in the final version since the balance of the essay will not be clear until it can be considered as a whole.

Preparation of material

It is intended that work on your essay will entail the use of reference books, magazines, newspapers, and other relevant material. Keep a careful record of all sources from which you obtain your information. Dates of newspapers and page numbers of books, with title, author, publisher, and date of publication must be noted if direct reference is made in the text. For example:

Shafto, T.A.C.: *Commerce: Structure and Practice*, p. 66, 2nd edition, McGraw-Hill, 1971.

Long quotations should be avoided or paraphrased. Tables of statistics, diagrams, and maps may be included if absolutely relevant, and should be incorporated into the text with a brief caption. Statistics may be placed in an appendix at the end of the essay.

Photographs and illustrations are better excluded unless they are vital, since they can give the essay the appearance of a scrap-book.

Preparation of the essay

At the beginning include a title page and, if necessary, on the next page a table of contents with page references. These additional pages are not themselves numbered.

The essay should be neatly written or typed on one side only of quarto paper; typing should be double-spaced with ample margins. Number the pages consecutively; do not number the pages of each section separately.

It is wise to enclose the essay in a cardboard cover to protect it from damage.

Bibliography

When you have completed your essay, compile a bibliography; this should contain details of the source of all material that has been of use to you in your work, including pamphlets, newspapers, and other information. A distinction should be made between those books which you have used, and those which offer further reading on the subject. The bibliography should be placed at the end of the essay.

Draft plans

The following pages contain examples of draft plans for the extended essay.

Banking in England
1. History of Banking
   Middle Ages to Present Day
2. The Bank of England
3. The Clearing Banks
4. The Services of a Bank:
   (a) Current accounts
   (b) Deposit accounts
   (c) Advances
   (d) Recurring payments
   (e) Night safes
   (f) Power of attorney
   (g) Safe custody
   (h) Income tax
   (i) Overseas business
   (j) Foreign travel
   (k) Wills and trusts
   (l) Economic information
   (m) Stocks and shares
   (n) Trader's credit
5. Bibliography

Hanson, J. L.: *A Textbook of Economics*, 5th edition, MacDonald & Evans, 1970.
Saw, R.: *The Bank of England*, Harrap, 1944.
Sayers, R. S.: *Modern Banking*, Clarendon Press, 1967.
Thorne, W. J.: *Banking*, 2nd edition, Oxford University Press, 1962.

Barclays Bank and its Services.
The National Westminster Bank: A Short Account of its Many Services.
Copy of Bank of England Return.

The book trade in England
1. Introduction
   (a) Brief history of books
   (b) Beginning of the trade
   (c) Invention of printing and paper-making
   (d) Engraving
   (e) Licences
   (f) Illustrations
2. Production
   (a) Paper

      (b) Printing
      (c) Colour printing
      (d) Binding
3. Publishing
      (a) Editorial Department
      (b) Copyright
      (c) Laws of libel, obscenity, violence
      (d) Books on commission
      (e) Literary agent
4. Bookselling
      (a) The economics of bookselling
      (b) Buying: Sale or return
                    See safe
                      On consignment
                      On approval
5. Miscellaneous
      (a) Booksellers' Clearing House
      (b) Book tokens
      (c) Advertising and publicity
      (d) National Book Sale
      (e) Net Book Agreement
6. Bibliography

Lehmann-Haupt, Helmut: *The Life of a Book*, Abelard-Schumann, 1957.
Unwin, Philip: *The Business of Books*, World Book Fair Catalogue, 1964.
Lane, Sir Allen: *The Growth of the Paperback*, ibid.
Joy, Thomas: *The Truth about Bookselling*, Pitman, 1964.

      7. Further reading

Dakers, Andrew: *Publishing*, Hale, 1961.
Mumby, F. A.: *Publishing and Bookselling*, Cape, 1956.
Plant, Marjorie: *The English Book Trade*, Allen & Unwin, 1966.
Clair, Colin: *A History of Printing in Britain*, Cassell, 1966.

    British Railways
1. History of railways in Britain
2. Growth of Government regulations
3. British Railways Act, 1921
4. Inter-war period and Second World War
5. Nationalization. Transport Act, 1947
6. Bibliography

The Reshaping of British Railways, H.M.S.O., 1963.
Ellis, Hamilton: *British Railways History, Volumes I and II*, Allen & Unwin, 1954, 1959.
Gwilliam, K. M.: *Transport and Public Policy*, Allen & Unwin, 1964.
Pamphlets from British Railways Public Relations Department and Railway Records Office.

7. Further reading

Milne, A.M. *The Economics of Inland Transport*, 2nd edition, Pitman, 1968.
Savage, C.: *The Economic History of Transport*, Hutchison, 1966.
Sherrington, C. E. R.: *100 Years of Inland Transport (1830–1933)*, F. Cass, 1969.

EXERCISES

Essays on the varied selection of the following topics should be written throughout the course.
1. Music for the cinema.
2. Youth clubs.
3. The causes of industrial strikes.
4. The influence of advertisements.
5. The perils of hire purchase.
6. 'Lack of money is the root of all evil' (George Bernard Shaw).
7. The moon.
8. Road behaviour is an indication of character.
9. Noise.
10. The advantages and disadvantages of co-education.
11. The modern police force.
12. The tyranny of the motor car.
13. A holiday at home.
14. Contentment is the enemy of progress.
15. The work of a great painter, musician, or dramatist.
16. Society today is too animal-conscious. Discuss.
17. The causes of juvenile crime.
18. Modern architecture.
19. The use and abuse of atomic power.
20. The care of old people.
21. Speaking in public.
22. The value of evening classes.
23. Reading in bed.
24. The future of Germany.

25. The rival attractions of theatre and cinema.
26. The House of Lords. What useful function can it perform today?
27. Preservation v. Redevelopment.
28. The world without sound.
29. Television as an educational medium.
30. Superstition.
31. The profitable use of leisure.
32. Next year.
33. The problems of mental health.
34. Changes in the status of women.
35. The power of the National Press.
36. Gambling.
37. The future of the United Nations.
38. On choosing a career.
39. Politics and international trade.
40. Industrial relations.
41. The rush hour. What practical methods could be introduced to improve the present situation in our cities?
42. Television advertising.
43. Fox-hunting.
44. Capital punishment. What grounds are there for its reintroduction for certain crimes?
45. How far ought Britain to limit immigration?
46. Automation and its effect on management and labour.
47. A sense of humour.
48. Middle-class values.
49. The tyranny of fashion.
50. The freedom of the Press.
51. The Arts should be state-subsidized. Discuss.
52. Penal reform.
53. The future of South-East Asia.
54. Alcohol and the motorist.
55. The export drive.
56. A critical account of my education.
57. Monarchy.
58. The 'Do-it-yourself' movement.
59. The value of examinations. What alternatives could be used to the traditional forms of assessment?
60. The future of the trade unions.
61. The National Health Service.
62. 'He has spent his life best, who has enjoyed it most' (Samuel Butler).

63. The censorship of literature and plays.
64. The preservation of wild-life in Britain.
65. The Channel tunnel. What are the economic and strategic consequences likely to be from its construction?
66. The value of public opinion polls.
67. The world problem of food production.
68. The role of the United States in the world today.
69. Nationalization of industry. Is this a discredited ideology?
70. Home decorating.
71. A radical change in the treatment of criminals is required. Discuss.
72. The future of the railways in Britain.
73. My favourite modern author.
74. The folly of the space race.
75. Keeping up with the Joneses.
76. 'The true welfare state teaches people how to stand on their own feet, not to live with their hands in the pockets of each other' (Dr. Erhard).
77. Sunday.
78. 'Education is what remains when we have forgotten all that we have been taught' (Marquis of Halifax).
79. The future of the Commonwealth.
80. The Prime Minister.
81. The British climate.
82. A woman's place is in the home.
83. Civil disobedience.
84. The greatest social evil of our time.
85. Saturday afternoon.
86. The value of consumer research.
87. Collecting things.
88. 'He who can does; he who cannot teaches' (Shaw).
89. Practical jokes.
90. The preservation of the countryside.
91. World population control.
92. Why do American tourists visit Britain?
93. Telepathy.
94. The importance of trees.
95. 'Moderation in the affairs of the nation is the highest virtue' (President Johnson).
96. A room of one's own.
97. Smuggling.
98. Family life today.

5. Interpreting written communication

The importance of comprehension

During the course of a normal working day an employee in the business world will have to deal with many 'pieces of paper'. These will include letters, memoranda, reports, circulars, etc. A busy employee has not the time to study all these papers in detail, yet he needs to know immediately what they contain. How can he assimilate this knowledge quickly and efficiently?

The answer is, of course, that he can achieve this rapid assimilation only through practice. He must learn to pick out the salient points of an argument quickly. Having recognized these points, he must be able to understand and interpret them. The comprehension exercise is designed to train the prospective employee to do just this. For this reason the questions set usually concern the meaning of particular words and phrases, explanations of sentences, and the interpretation of particular points, such as the author's intention or attitude. It is not a test of general knowledge but the ability to assimilate and interpret given facts. In all cases answers must be based on what the author says in the passage. How, then, should you set about a comprehension exercise?

Prepare carefully

Read the passage once or twice in order to grasp the theme and the author's attitude towards the subject. If the meaning is clear, read through the questions and relate them to the passage itself, locating the exact lines to which they refer.

Answering the questions

General hints

Preciseness is the criterion for answering comprehension questions. The two common faults are a failure to give complete answers and an inability to discriminate between relevant and irrelevant material. Both these arise from a careless reading of either the passage or the questions or a tendency to generalize when precise details are required.

Make certain that every requirement of the question has been covered by your answer. Search the passage carefully for any factors which may throw light upon your answer.

Have the courage to delete points which digress from the question or are a repetition of what has already been stated.

Word explanation

The explanation of words and short phrases from the passage need not be set out in sentence form. The given words must be written down first followed by a single word or short phrase giving the meaning. Make certain that you explain the words *as they are used in the passage*. Always consider each word in its context since its meaning in the passage may well differ from its usual sense.

The single word or phrase chosen to replace the given word must have *exactly* the same meaning as the original; an approximate equivalent is valueless.

Do not give a selection of words in the hope that one is correct. The examiner will mark the first one only.

Check that the explanation retains the same part of speech as the given word. This can be verified by substituting the new word or phrase for the original in the passage. An accidental alteration of syntax will be evident at once. Thus an adjective must be defined by using another adjective or adjectival phrase.

Interpretation

All other questions should be answered in sentence form and in your own words unless you are asked to quote from the passage.

Where an explanation of a long phrase or sentence is asked for, a mere subsitution of words in the form of a paraphrase may not *explain* the meaning. Take each phrase separately and interpret the implication of every word.

Do not ignore the context of such questions. Look at the sentences either side of the one for explanation since the train of thought which the author presents will have a bearing on that sentence.

Assessment

A question which begins 'Comment on the author's use of ... ' does not require criticism of the writer. You should endeavour to explain why the author has used a certain style or phrase in order to convey his ideas.

An appraisal of the author's opinions must be based entirely on the arguments he presents in the given passage. Any assessment of character must be supported by evidence.

Check your work

When the answers are complete, examine the questions again and read the passage once more to confirm that all relevant details have been included in the answers.

Finally check the spelling of words from the original which have been retained in the answers you have written.

Worked example

As each new traffic 'improvement' is advertised by a smug local authority placard we pedestrians snarl. They are only thinking of the motorist. The faster the brute can drive his car the worse off we are. 'New Pedestrian subway', says the same placard. So that is where we are supposed to go. Down in a dank hole under Marble 5
Arch, Victoria, Hyde Park Corner, or wherever it is. Meanwhile the motorist lords it over London—desecrating the park, smoking out pedestrians from the canyons of office blocks, shouting to heaven with the intolerable roar of his engine and the shrill cry of his horn. 10

The only answer to this is to fight back. As pedestrians we know

how effective a guerrilla war can be to harass the enemy. A swift rush just as the lights go green; in-fighting in a busy shopping street; a sudden explosion of pedestrians, like a Molotov-cocktail, across
15 the front of a car moving through a narrow defile. Now we know what Wellington's Peninsular irregulars felt as they smote Napoleon's serried ranks. Given a few years of training in these techniques of obstruction, the pedestrian might run the motorist out of central London.
20 Once we are seated in a car, however, an odd change comes over us. From being an ugly little four-wheeler, the car has become as beautiful and as responsive as a hunting cheetah. Down goes the accelerator and with a musical crackle of exhaust we fly through the shopping centre. Pedestrians (too shaken to fight back, poor fools)
25 bolt for the safety of the subways. That is where they belong. Oh, the marvellous exultation of the motor age! It is not that we want to drive fast (nor indeed do we get a chance). But what a sense of superiority the car confers even in the hour-long traffic jam.

Thus a state of schizophrenia is induced by the motor age; as
30 pedestrians we revile what we exult in as motorists. How will it all be resolved? There are dizzy prospects of the two-level city. Here pedestrians would be isolated from the gross world of the motor car by a raised deck. Down below cars can roar their engines and blow their horns to their hearts' content, but they will have no game to
35 hunt. From the motorists' point of view, all the world will be a road. Parks, temples, theatres—nothing will stand in the way of the triumphant motor car. It will go under with the effortless ease of a mole. No matter if life will seem a little dull for some of the pedestrians, as they loll about in the car-free precincts. Like Wellington's
40 veterans, they will be sustained by the thought of their heroic actions in the past.

Times Educational Supplement.

Questions

(a) Give briefly the meaning of the following words as they are used in the passage:
smug (line 1)   dank (line 5)   desecrating (line 7)
irregulars (line 16)   revile (line 30).
(b) Explain the meaning of the following phrases:
guerrilla war (line 12)   serried ranks (line 17).
(c) Why is the word 'canyons' appropriate for the description of office blocks?

(d) How is a state of schizophrenia induced by the motor age?
(e) What kind of city of the future does the author envisage?
(f) How will this plan affect the pedestrian?

Answers

(a) smug: self-satisfied
    dank: unpleasantly damp
    desecrating: spoiling
    irregulars: conscripts
    revile: abuse.
(b) A guerrilla war is one which is fought by a small group of people against a larger force.
    Serried ranks are troops drawn up closely in lines.
(c) 'Canyons' is an appropriate word used to described blocks of offices since these buildings resemble canyons in a number of ways. The passages between them are narrow, the sides are vertical and the only sign of movement is at the base where streams of traffic look like rivers. In addition these office blocks suggest the arid climate of the deserts in which canyons are found.
(d) A state of schizophrenia in the motor age arises from the conflicting feelings which most people possess. When they are motorists they loathe pedestrians, but as soon as they become pedestrians, instantly they alter their attitude, and loathe the motorists.
(e) The author sees the city of the future built on two levels, the pedestrians raised above and segregated from the motor cars below.
(f) The pedestrians will be safe from the menace of road-traffic, but they may find life somewhat dull. However, they will be able to endure this quieter life with memories of the time when they waged war against the motor-car.

EXERCISES

1. Hannah, on the contrary, demanded no respect—only flattery; if her admirers only *told* her that she was an angel, she would let them *treat* her as an idiot. So very credulous and frivolous was she; so very silly did she become when besieged with attention, flattered and admired to the proper degree, that there were moments when 5 Helstone actually felt tempted to commit matrimony a second time,

and to try the experiment of taking her for his second helpmeet; but, fortunately, the salutary recollection of the ennuis of his first marriage, the impression still left on him of the weight of the mill-
10 stone he had once worn round his neck, the fixity of his feeling respecting the insufferable evils of conjugal existence, operated as a check to his tenderness, suppressed the sigh heaving his old iron lungs, and restrained him from whispering to Hannah proposals it would have been high fun and great satisfaction to her to hear.
15 It is probable she would have married him if he had asked her; her parents would have quite approved the match; to them his fifty-five years, his bend-leather heart, could have presented no obstacles; and, as he was a rector, held an excellent living, occupied a good house, and was supposed even to have private property, her
20 parents, I say, would have delivered Hannah over to his loving kindness and his tender mercies without one scruple; and the second Mrs. Helstone, inversing the natural order of insect existence, would have fluttered through the honeymoon a bright, admired butterfly, and crawled the rest of her days a sordid, trampled worm.

Shirley, Charlotte Brontë.

(1) Give the meaning of the following words as they are used in the passage:
credulous (line 3)   salutary (line 8)   ennuis (line 8).
(2) What prevented Helstone from marrying for a second time?
(3) Why would Hannah have married Helstone if he had asked her?
(4) What reasons would Hannah's parents have for approving the marriage?
(5) What do we learn of the character of Helstone from this passage?

2. It was the Centenary of the establishment of Sunday Schools. Edwin hated Sunday Schools. Nay, he venomously resented them, though they had long since ceased to incommode him. They were connected in his memory with atrocious tedium, pietistic insincerity,
5 and humiliating contacts. At the bottom of his mind he still regarded them as a malicious device of parents for wilfully harassing and persecuting inoffensive, helpless children. And he had a particular grudge against them because he alone of his father's offspring had been chosen for the nauseating infliction. Why should his sisters
10 have been spared and he doomed? He became really impatient when Sunday Schools were under discussion, and from mere

irrational annoyance he would not admit that Sunday Schools had any good qualities whatever. He knew nothing of their history, and wished to know nothing.

Nevertheless, when the day of Centenary dawned—and dawned in splendour—he was compelled, even within himself, to treat Sunday Schools with more consideration. And, in fact, for two or three days previously the gathering force of public opinion had been changing his attitude from stern hatred to a sort of half-hearted derision. Now, the derision was mysteriously transformed into an inimical respect. By what? By he knew not what. By something without a name in the air which the mind breathes. He felt it at six o'clock, ere he arose. Lying in bed he felt it. The day was to be a festival. The shop would not open, nor the printing office. The way of daily life would be quite changed. He was free—that was, nearly free. He said to himself that of course his excited father would expect him to witness the celebrations and to wear his best clothes, and that was a bore. But therein he was not quite honest. For he secretly wanted to witness the celebrations and to wear his best clothes. His curiosity was hungry. He admitted, what many had been asserting for weeks, that the Centenary was going to be a big thing; and his social instinct wished him to share in the pride of it.

Clayhanger, Arnold Bennett.

(1) Give briefly the meaning of the following words and phrases as they are used in the passage:
venomously (line 2)   incommode (line 3)   atrocious
tedium (line 4)   pietistic insincerity (line 4)   irrational (line 12)   inimical (line 20).
(2) What were the root causes of Edwin's dislike of Sunday Schools?
(3) What does one learn from this extract of the character of Edwin's father?
(4) What forces caused Edwin to alter his attitude towards the Sunday School centenary?

3.   THE MALAGASY REPUBLIC
Agriculture
Cattle-raising could make an important contribution to economic development, there being an estimated 8 million animals of the *zebu* type in the country. However, because these animals are regarded as symbols of wealth and status rather than a subject for economic

5 exploitation, there has been virtually no scientific breeding. There are, however, substantial exports of frozen and canned meat to France and Reunion.

The most important export product is coffee, accounting for 31·5 per cent of total exports. Production, which includes a large per-
10 centage of *robusta* (a type of coffee mainly used for blending and *instant*), is not expected to develop beyond the country's exportable quota, at present fixed at 50,000 tons, and local consumption estimated at 5,000 tons.

Sugar exports have suffered from the loss of the privileged position
15 which Malagasy sugar formerly enjoyed in France. It is hoped that the damage will be at least partly repaired by the creation of a common market in sugar by the O.C.A.M. (*Organisation Commune Africaine & Malagasy*) of which the Malagasy Republic is a member.

More intensive cultivation of rice, which is the country's staple
20 food, is one of the Government's primary concerns. The aim is to reach a production of 2 million tons of paddy in order to feed a population growing at the rate of 2·7 per cent; and at the same time to increase exports of high grade rice to Europe.

Other major exports include vanilla, sisal, tobacco, cloves, raffia,
25 butter beans, graphite, hides and skins, ground-nuts and pepper.

The export to European markets of bananas cultivated on the east coast is expanding satisfactorily; and a vast cotton growing project in the south is making progress.

>*Hints to Businessmen visiting the Malagasy Republic* (1967). Reprinted by permission of the Controller of Her Majesty's Stationery Office.

Answer the following questions based on the above passage. Where an answer cannot be obtained from the information given, write 'not stated'.

(1) What is the principal export of the Malagasy Republic?
(2) To whom does she export (a) meat; (b) rice; (c) bananas; (d) cloves?
(3) What problem faces the economic development of cattle rearing?
(4) Is coffee production expanding?
(5) What is the population of the Malagasy Republic?
(6) What set-back have the sugar exports encountered?
(7) How is this to be overcome?
(8) What is the population growth-rate?
(9) Which product is grown extensively in the south?

(10) What is robusta?
(11) How much coffee is produced annually?
(12) Where on the island are bananas grown?
(13) What is the principal food of the Republic?
(14) Which of the following products are exported from the Malagasy Republic: sisal, wheat, vanilla, pepper, tea, tobacco, lead, fruit?

4.   THE DISCOVERY OF EXPLOSIVES AT LIVERPOOL

Commenting on the above subject, *The Times* enters into full details of the consignment of infernal machines from America to England, and assumes that the explosive material they contained was either intended for the destruction of public buildings in this country, or to excite feelings of uneasiness and apprehension. It hopes that the Government will be able to discover full particulars of the plot and plotters, and thinks there is no doubt that the authorities in America can be relied upon to co-operate in the enquiries now being made. The whole business is attributable directly to the American Fenian leaders whose platform utterances have excited the more coarse and brutal members of that organisation. Although all vigilance must be used against the designs of the agitators, it will not do to give way to panic, and there is comfort in thinking that the crimes contemplated will produce such a feeling as may baffle the designs of the conspirators.

The *Daily News* will not be so rash or inconsiderate as to minimize the dangers attendant upon the importation of the machines, and it differs from the Home Secretary as to the best means of dealing with the kind of warfare they were intended to wage. Instead of interfering with free discussion as a preventive against conspiracies, our contemporary inclines to the view that indulgence in even the strongest invective and denunciation acts as a safety-valve and relieves the pressure which, otherwise, might break forth into direct crime. Speculation as to the exact connection between the writers in such prints as the *Irish World* of New York, and the actual persons importing the infernal machines, would at present be useless, but America will not refuse to join in the inquiries on the subject which are already in progress.

The affair must be looked fully in the face and all needful steps be taken to ensure safety, or, the *Daily Chronicle* thinks, there may be some terrible disaster, because men do not spend their money

upon infernal machines unless they intend to use them. The 'brave words which came by post and telegraph from the other side of the Atlantic' are indications of the intentions of the senders, and there
35 is no mistaking the real malignity of their motives. The *Chronicle* approves of the Home Secretary's views on the subject of seditious language, and holds that the Government has done its duty in calling the attention of the authorities at Washington to the speeches and writings of the American Fenians.

London Evening News, 26th July, 1881.

(1) Explain what each of the following words and phrases means in its context in the passage:
consignment of infernal machines (line 2)
our contemporary (line 20)   invective (line 22)
prints (line 25)   malignity (line 35)
seditious language (line 36).

(2) Using your own words, rewrite the sentence which begins, 'Although all vigilance must be used ...' (lines 11–15).

(3) What is the meaning of the phrase 'to minimize the dangers attendant upon the importation of the machines' (lines 16–17)?

(4) In what way do the views of the *Daily Chronicle* regarding the discovery of explosives differ from those of the *Daily News*?

5. The way to the wood is by Back Lane, at the mouth of which stands a notice saying *No Through Road*. I am not over-fond of signs and notices as a general rule, especially such as are hortatory and prohibitive, but this one says just about the most encouraging
5 and companionable thing a sign can say.

It means that you can amble down Back Lane towards the wood in a state of tolerable dreaminess without being edged into the ditch by motors. And in the banks and hedges of Back Lane you can always find snowdrops and aconites a-flowering before you see
10 them anywhere else. Perhaps they, too, prefer the peace of a lane that is sacred to feet and hooves.

Now the bone-bare architecture of the landscape appeals to a cool, dry taste. Now you can see how the small things live, more clearly than when their passionate, anonymous little lives are masked
15 from view by the profusion of summer. They live tremulously, precariously, yet with a perfect confidence and self-possession, in obedience to the inexorable rule of Nature, which is the only law that they, being unmetaphysical, know.

Yet within the iron collar of necessity the creatures express delight. Who can doubt it that has watched a flock of starlings wheel and swoop and soar on the resilient air, in mid-morning on a fine day when they have breakfasted well? All birds, or almost all, express happiness at times, taking the air in congenial congregations for no material purpose that one can discern, dancing and playing together and simply enjoying the power of flight, the sweetness of life.

Even rooks flying over the common seem to loll and dream as they ride the mild clear airs towards the wood. When the mild days come in winter you can almost sense the relief and exhilaration of the creatures. And if you enter the wood quietly and sit on a fallen tree while the shock of your invasion wears off, life soon begins to stir around you.

How many mice live in the wood? In winter you see them peeping hesitantly out from the mosses and the ivy, stepping delicately through grass and bracken which is itself forest-high to them. Odd to think how a mouse must see the world. Even if you lay your head on the earth, your eyes are still many times higher than a mouse's. Impossible to imagine how tall a cat must seem to a mouse.

If dusk is falling as you walk back from the wood you will notice how the small birds come together at evening. There are companies of finches and bands of sparrows. The hedgerow is alive with their twittering.

Most birds are companionable creatures. It is impossible to know if friends come together after a day's labours, or if one bird is as congenial as another to a bird of like kind. However that may be, there they are, chirruping and gossiping in little companies which suddenly rise and fly twittering over the common, threes and fours and fives together, towards the great barns and farmyards where they will spend the night, snug in the stacks.

Sometimes as I emerge from Back Lane a cat will materialize out of the shadows near the sign that says *No Through Road*. He is one of a family of curious cats that enjoy walking out with people, as if they were dogs. He and I will pad quietly back to the old cottage in a companionable silence. No point in telling him what I have seen. He knows it all much better than I.

J. Robertson Glasgow, *Sunday Times*.

(1) Give the meaning of the following words as they are used in the passage:
   hortatory (line 3)   tolerable (line 7)   profusion (line 15)

tremulously (line 15)   precariously (line 16)   inexorable (line 17)   unmetaphysical (line 18)   resilient (line 21)   congenial (line 23)   exhilaration (line 29).

(2) Why does the author consider that the sign 'No Through Road' says 'just about the most encouraging and companionable thing a sign can say'?

(3) Explain the apparent contradiction contained in the sentence, 'They live tremulously, precariously, yet with a perfect confidence and self-possession' (lines 15-16).

(4) What human characteristics does the author attribute to the creatures in the way he describes their behaviour?

(5) Quote four figures of speech used in this passage.

6.   CONCERT PROMOTION

In recent years, it has become plain that the members of all four orchestras are dependent for a substantial part of their incomes on their orchestras giving a sufficient number of public concerts. The difficulty is that with very few exceptions concerts do not and cannot pay. The result is that few concerts are today promoted by commercial impresarios at their own risk. Occasionally a concert is financed by an aspirant soloist or conductor, or the orchestra is engaged for a charity performance, and a number of concerts are promoted by choral and other musical organizations. But for the most part concerts are promoted by the orchestras themselves. This cannot be done without substantial subsidies. The amount varies according to the venue, but in the case of the Royal Festival Hall an average of at least £1,200 per concert must be provided.

In our view these subsidies must be accepted as the price a great city must pay to provide a proper range of music for its citizens and visitors. This is a public service. But we also think it necessary to affirm the principle, sometimes lost sight of in discussions of this problem, that public funds should be used to provide services for the public and not merely to create employment. In other words, the supply of music must be related to the demand. This does not necessarily mean that a concert must be justifiable on commercial grounds. A concert of high artistic standard given to a good audience is properly satisfying a demand even if it involves a substantial charge to public funds. The same may be said of a concert which attracts a smaller audience but supplies a more specialized demand and is therefore justifiable on artistic grounds. But we cannot help feeling that in some cases concerts have been promoted without being justifiable on either commercial or artistic grounds, their main *raison d'être* being to provide work for the members of the orchestra. In any event, it is an obligation to the public purse to be sure that concert promotion involving heavy public subsidies is undertaken by a person or body with great musical knowledge and experience and a high sense of responsibility.

If concerts are to be supported out of public funds it is also necessary that their programmes should be properly co-ordinated. A few years ago the arrangement of programmes in London was deplorably haphazard. There was much duplication and waste. But we were pleased to notice that much has recently been done towards ensuring that clashes are avoided and a wider choice made available to the concert-going public. We refer in particular to the committee set up to co-ordinate the programmes of three orchestras and to the successful introduction of a ticket voucher scheme by the General Manager of the Royal Festival Hall. We are of opinion that for the reasons set out in this and the preceding paragraph a permanent co-ordinating machinery should be set up to include all four orchestras, and we make recommendations to this effect.

The Goodman Report on London Orchestras, 1965.

(1) Give the meaning of the following words as they are used in the passage:
   impresarios (line 6)   aspirant (line 7)   venue (line 12)
   raison d'être (line 29).
(2) How should public funds be spent on the promotion of concerts?
(3) In what way is concert promotion in London a public service?
(4) When is it justifiable to subsidize a concert which is not a financial success?
(5) Who at present promote concerts in London?
(6) What are the two major criticisms of concert promotion in London on which this report comments?
(7) What recommendations are made in this report regarding concert promotion?

7. The debate in the House of Commons last night on the Transvaal retrocession discovered nothing that was not known, excepting the defence which the Government made, and which was looked forward to by a large section of the Liberal party with some anxiety. The charge the Opposition had to make against the Government was plain and clear, and it was sustained in an able and on the whole fair speech by Sir Michael Hicks-Beach. For reasons which were disputed at the time, the late Government annexed the Transvaal,

and proceeded upon the ordinary lines to secure the allegiance of
10 the inhabitants which they had assumed, upon what seemed trustworthy but which proved to be misleading evidence, was a peaceful and an easy matter. The present Government came into power, and, in the face of their adverse opinions respecting the policy of their predecessors, proceeded loyally to build upon the foundations that
15 had been laid. In the Speech from the Throne last January it was announced to the discomfiture of the Boers, who were agitating for independence and expecting much from the Liberal Government, that the Queen's authority would be vindicated. Up to this point there is no disagreement between the Government and the Op-
20 position. But, continues the indictment of the ex-Colonial Secretary, for some inexplicable reason, which Sir H. Holland recognised as the combined effect of Radical pressure and military defeats, the Government, after the disaster of Majuba Hill and its two unfortunate predecessors, concluded a peace, and handed back the
25 country to the victorious farmers. There is considerable strength in such a representation, and there is no use in denying the fact that immediately after cessation of hostilities there was in the country a great deal of irritation consequent upon a sense of wounded pride. But the answer of the Government covered the whole ground and
30 was complete. It contradicted the indictment upon an important allegation and explained the retrocession upon the very grounds upon which the country was taken over by the late Government. The contradiction was, that overtures for peace were commenced before either of the three disasters occurred. On the 10th and 26th
35 January, Lord Kimberley wrote that if armed opposition ceased Her Majesty's Government would endeavour to frame such a scheme as in their belief would satisfy all intelligent friends of the Transvaal. The first of the three 'unhappy engagements' of Sir George Colley did not take place until January 27th. The motive of the Govern-
40 ment for the cessation of the war could not therefore have been the triple disaster to our arms.

London Evening News, 26th July, 1881.

(1) Explain briefly the meaning of the following words as they are used in the passage:
retrocession (line 2)   indictment (line 20)
representation (line 26)   cessation of hostilities (line 27).
(2) Was the Liberal Party the Government or the Opposition at this time?
(3) Was the previous Government a Liberal one?

(4) What accusation did the Opposition bring against the Government in their handling of the Transvaal situation?
(5) What answer did the Government give to this accusation?
(6) Who at this time were in control of the Transvaal?
(7) What is the significance of the word 'intelligent' as used in line 37?
(8) What were the 'three unhappy engagements'?

8. CHEAPER ACROSS THE ATLANTIC

The scheduled airlines have at last accepted the fact that people in North America and in Europe, with more leisure and higher standards of living, want cheaper fares for journeys across the Atlantic. In spite of one contrary vote at the International Air Transport Association conference in Montreal the public will be able, from 5 February 1 next year, to buy a return ticket on a regular flight between London and New York for £79.50 as long as they book three months in advance. It is a facility which is long overdue.

British Overseas Airways Corporation is right to say that it will not be balked in its plan to introduce this 'Early Bird' fares concept 10 because one vote out of 39 was cast against it. The single dissenter, Lufthansa, is worried that the proposed rates would be too complex and unprofitable, but its Atlantic operations, as well as those of most of the other major airlines, have not shown a profit recently. BOAC is at least proposing a constructive way of relieving the situation. The 15 airlines should make an effort to unlock the era of mass travel and to fill the hundreds of thousands of empty seats which they are now flying around in their jumbo jet fleets. If the BOAC rate is found not to work after a fair trial there would then be grounds for raising it.

In the desperate economic circumstances in which the scheduled 20 airlines find themselves today almost any solution is worth trying. The charter carriers have gradually crept up on them, undermining their business on the Atlantic in particular with fares as low as £50 return for travellers prepared to join large groups. The point has now been reached where the charter airlines have begun to eat into 25 the business traffic which has been traditionally one of the major sources of high revenue for the scheduled operators. Now, although belatedly, the IATA airlines have climbed down from their high-fare policy, and it is the turn of the charter carriers to become worried.

The Times

As far as possible in your own words, answer the following questions:

(1) What factors have led to the decision for cheaper air fares?
(2) How will cheaper fares benefit the airlines?
(3) What conditions must travellers fulfil to benefit from the proposed cheaper fares?
(4) Which airline is not in favour of cheaper fares?
(5) What effect have charter flight companies on the major airlines?
(6) What effect will the proposed cheaper fares have on charter companies?
(7) Write in full the names of the organizations: B.O.A.C., I.A.T.A.
(8) How have charter flight companies been able to offer Atlantic return flights for only £50?

9.   THE IVORY COAST, NIGER AND UPPER VOLTA
Area and geographical features
The Ivory Coast covers an area of 127,000 square miles, and lies on the Gulf of Guinea. It is bordered in the west by Liberia and the Republic of Guinea, to the north by Mali and Upper Volta, and to the east by Ghana. The country is divided into two geographical areas
5 consisting of equatorial rain forests in the south to the drier and less humid savannah belt in the north.

Niger has an area of 459,000 square miles, and is bounded on the north by Algeria and by Libya, on the south by Nigeria, Dahomey and Upper Volta, on the east by Chad, and on the west by Mali. It
10 has no coastline but the River Niger flows for 185 miles through the south-western part of the country. For 6 months of the year, from October to March, the river can be navigated by small craft from the capital Niamey to the town of Gaya on the borders of Nigeria. The only other important mass of navigable water is a part of Lake Chad.
15 Cultivated land amounts to only 2 per cent of the total area and this is mostly concentrated in a strip some 100 miles broad running along the Nigerian frontier. The country is a vast plateau with a mean elevation of approximately 1,200 feet but a mountainous area in the centre has peaks of up to 6,000 feet and the massifs along the Libyan
20 border average about 2,600 feet. The north of the country is Saharan and the south is mostly savannah.

Upper Volta is a land-locked country covering an area of some 105,900 square miles. It is bounded on the north and west by Mali, on the north and east by Niger, and in the south by the Ivory Coast,
25 Ghana, Togo and Dahomey. It is about 500 miles from the sea and has no navigable rivers. The most important rivers are the Red, White and Black Voltas, but these become a trickle during the dry seasons. The Mossi plateau which covers almost the whole of the

country is a ferruginous crust unfavourable for agriculture. There are several small granite mounds of over 500 feet dotted unevenly through- 30 out the country. Climatic conditions are severe and there is a chronic shortage of water.

Answer the following questions based on the above passage. Where an answer cannot be obtained from the information given, write 'not stated'.
(1) Which of these countries has a coastline?
(2) In which general direction does Niger lie in relation to the Ivory Coast?
(3) Which part of the Niger River is navigable?
(4) Which rivers in Upper Volta are navigable?
(5) Which rivers in the Ivory Coast are navigable?
(6) Place the three countries in ascending order of size.
(7) What are the names of the capital cities of these countries?
(8) In which part of Niger is there agriculture?
(9) Why is there little agriculture in the Upper Volta?
(10) Which parts of Niger are mountainous?
(11) Compare the climatic conditions of these countries.
(12) Which part of Niger is desert?

Hints to Businessmen visiting the Ivory Coast, Niger and Upper Volta. Reprinted by permission of the Controller of Her Majesty's Stationery Office.

10. The executive you serve has asked you to read through this article and find out, if possible, the answers to the questions that follow. Write out all the numbers and answer those that can be answered; leave a blank against each number where no answer is possible.

WOODEN ROOFS

Since wood must be the oldest structural material used by man, it is odd to discover that by the application of a little science it can be made to do some quite new things.

At the Amersham laboratories of the Timber Development Association, some absorbing research on wooden roofs is in pro- 5 gress. By applying geometrical ideas first worked out in the nineteenth century, delicate wooden 'shells' can be constructed which roof in enormous areas, but need support only at a few points at the edge.

Similar roofs have been made in concrete on the Continent for a 10 few years, but this country is leading the way in the use of timber for shell roofs.

Apart from their wide and graceful spans with minimum supports, timber-shell roofs are lighter (reducing foundation costs), cheaper, and easier to erect.

They are now beginning to penetrate into architectural practice—for instance, the roofs of the new Oxford Road Station, Manchester, are being made in this way.

Three layers of wooden strips glued together form the 'shell'. The strips of one layer run at an angle to the next, in accordance with the geometry of the construction. More or less any kind of timber can be used.

The hope of the Timber Development Association is that this form of roof will be used increasingly for factories and other large industrial buildings. Timber-shell roofs, with their excellent insulation, cheapness, and wide spans, are ideally suited for such applications.

Some roofs are built in swinging geometric curves—such as 'hyperbolic paraboloids' and 'conoids'—in graceful contrast to the usual corregated asbestos.

(1) Are these roofs any good for keeping the cold out and heat in?
(2) Is there any advantage in foundation construction and for putting up the roofs?
(3) Are some of the roofs already in use in Belgium?
(4) Can we get a more artistic-looking roof by using wood?
(5) How long ago were these designs worked out?
(6) What seems to be the chief advantage of these roofs?
(7) Could plastics be used in the same way?
(8) Who is doing the spadework in finding out about these roofs?

Royal Society of Arts.

11. TAKING STOCK

Neville Cardus examines his critical equipment

It is a good thing if a critic (or anybody else) submits himself periodically to self-examination, to try to find out where he now stands, mentally and technically. Has he, over a period of the past few years, slipped, not kept up with the Joneses, and suffered a general feebling of his antennae? Myself, as I risk this self-stocktaking, am appalled to realize how little I know thoroughly (yet am astonished at how much I do know). The gaps in my store of knowledge are capacious. How did I presume to have the courage to undertake the onerous job of music critic for this journal nearly

forty years ago? Luckily then I didn't have the faintest notion of
the range of my ignorance. To this day I am constantly aware that
I go into action—that is, attend concerts—with vulnerable places
in my armour.

I imagined I had a fairly comprehensive view and experience of
Mahler's music until, having written a book about him, I have
read the reviews. Maybe, on the whole, I am not abnormally misinformed about the general background of so-called classical music.
What distresses me is my congenital blind spots. No matter how
intensively I have, over the years, applied myself to the study of
Bach, much of his music remains to me remote in aesthetic appeal,
and technically (God forgive me!) limited: a quick and a slow
movement, each often wonderful, but repetition seems to feed on
repetition. It is, of course, my terrible loss, but there it is—Bach is
for me not a musical or a spiritual necessity. Palestrina can touch
me on a tenderer spiritual spot (and I am neither a Catholic nor a
Protestant). It seems to me the narrowest old hat to pretend that,
either as musician or humanist, Bach is of the same stature as the
large-viewed and technically versatile and well-nigh flawless Mozart.

As I overhaul my catechism, as it involves the scene of music
today, my circle of knowledge and experience naturally diminishes;
worse still, if actual 'blind spots' are not in the increase, there is
definitely an increase of astigmatism and myopia. Apparently I am
the only music critic in London at the moment who can't sit down at
will and read the score of Schoenberg's *Moses and Aaron*. My vision
is so distorted that I am unable to see perpetual and infallible
genius daily or nightly on view at an Aldeburgh Festival. Britten,
being human, is bound to some display of error (and, in my opinion,
is all the more interesting a composer because of recurrent visitations
of mortal frailty). I doubt if Mozart himself was not only the most
divinely gifted composer of his period but also the most gifted pianist,
piano accompanist, conductor, and turner-over of the music copy.

Possibly I am heretical beyond the pale about Britten. And here I
might point out that I fancy I was the first—at any rate, one of the
first—critics to draw attention to the talent of Benjamin Britten in
this newspaper, in a review of a *Ballad of Heroes*, played at a
'festival of music for the people' in London in 1939. I also chanced
applying the word 'genius' to the cycle *Les Illuminations* the first
time it was performed. I am not at all sure (and here I see the sky
darkening with the arrows of my assailants) that Britten has quite
realized the promise of those early years culminating in *Peter Grimes*.
There have been deepenings, of course, of his musical mind and

nature. But does the art of his music, the sheer inspiration, flash as originally, as spontaneously, as during those first creative moments? The *War Requiem*, I know, is a deeply moving music-
55 poetic experience, enhanced by extra-musical associations. If I were pressed into a corner, I would maintain that for absolutely unique Britten the *Variations on a Theme of Purcell* want a lot of beating. This, I suspect, is my most unforgivable heresy. As a matter of fact I am too great an admirer of Britten, too conscious of the
60 variable flows of genius, its ups and downs and short circuitings to wish to ally myself with the uncritical hosts of the Britten incense-bearers. *The Guardian.*

(1) Give the meaning of the following words as they are used in the passage:
capacious (line 8)   onerous (line 9)   aesthetic (line 20)
catechism (line 29)   infallible (line 35)   culminating (line 50)   enhanced (line 55).
(2) What differences does the author see in himself as a critic today compared with himself 40 years ago?
(3) Explain the meaning of the phrase 'Has he ... slipped, not kept up with the Joneses, and suffered a general feebling of his antennae?' (lines 3–5).
(4) What are 'congenital blind spots' for a music critic?
(5) What does the author mean by the phrase, 'there is definitely an increase of astigmatism and myopia' (lines 31–32)?
(6) In your own words, explain the meaning of the following phrases:
    (i) recurrent visitations of mortal frailty (lines 38–39);
    (ii) beyond the pale (line 42).
(7) In what way can a music critic 'overhaul his catechism'?

12.
On 11 May 1559 John Knox, a revolutionary priest imbued with the theology of Calvin's Geneva, preached a sermon 'vehement against idolatry' in the ancient and beautiful church of St. John in Perth. As a result of this, a mob of those whom Knox at the time referred to as
5 'the brethren' and some years later as 'the rascal multitude' damaged the ornaments in the kirk, and then rushed out to sack the houses of the Grey and Black Friars, and the Carthusian monastery. The infuriated Queen Regent, Mary of Guise, ordered government troops to muster at Stirling before marching to Perth to punish the
10 preacher and the burgesses. Knox and his friends in turn called up an army of nobles and lairds from the corners of the Lowlands styling

themselves 'the Faithful Congregation of Christ Jesus in Scotland' and they prepared to wield 'the sword in just defence' against the crown. In a country too often bedevilled by faction, rebellion was not a novelty: and the Regent could not but notice that all her personal enemies were ranged with the heretics. But this time there was much more at stake than the desire of one aristocratic clique to thrust another from power. This was a great popular revolution backed by a large number of articulate men of every class discontented with the political and religious environment in which they lived. And the outcome of the struggle which began at Perth had the most profound effects upon Scottish society. Before it, Scotland had been a Catholic country with peculiarly close links to Rome for five hundred years. After it, the Scottish Parliament declared the country Protestant and independent of Rome—and so it remained in following centuries. Before it, Scotland had been for a decade the pawn of France; but this itself was merely an extreme consequence of the hostility which had prevailed between England and Scotland for 250 years. After it, England became Scotland's firm ally, and the stage was set for the gradual integration of Britain which was to result first in the Unions of 1603 and 1707, and then to grow stronger with every decade until in the twentieth century the survival of national identity itself appeared endangered to Scots of many different political persuasions. In Scotland the medieval world began to die with the Reformation: the modern world began to be born.

A History of the Scottish People 1560–1830, T. C. Smout (Collins).

(1) Using a single word or short phrase, explain the meaning of the following words in the passage:
imbued (line 1)   kirk (line 6)   Regent (line 8)
burgesses (line 10)   heretics (line 16)   clique (line 17)
articulate (line 19)   peculiarly (line 23).

(2) What fundamental change came to Scotland as a result of the actions of John Knox and his followers?

(3) In your own words explain the meaning of the phrase 'vehement against idolatry' (lines 2–3).

(4) What did Knox imply in descriptions he gave of his followers firstly as 'the brethren' and later as 'the rascal multitude'?

(5) What is meant by the statement 'Scotland had been for a decade the pawn of France' (line 26)?

(6) What problems did Mary of Guise face when she attempted to suppress the rebellion started in Perth?

(7) Explain the description of Scotland as 'a country too often bedevilled by faction' (line 14).
(8) How has the relationship between Scotland and England changed from the time of Knox to the present day?

6. Summarizing written communication

The importance of summarizing in business

Everyday the quantity of correspondence and other written information which managers receive is enormous. Since there is a limit to what even the most efficient executive can read, summaries are frequently required so that the management can save time by reading a shortened version which retains only the main points of the original article.

The purpose of a summary or précis is to present the salient points of a given passage in a more concise form so that the essential ideas are easily and quickly understood. In this respect the précis is primarily a test of comprehension which leads to an exercise in expression and style.

In English examinations many candidates attempt the précis with no clear idea of how this question should be approached. They assume that instinct and chance will lead them to a successful summary of the passage which is set. This lack of method is the greatest time-waster and candidates who do not know how a précis should be planned seldom produce a satisfactory version.

There are a number of methods of précis writing, all related in basic principles and each having its own merits according to the character of the passage to be condensed.

Preparation

(a) Read the passage through once. If the main theme is not clear, read the passage again. Should the meaning still be difficult to grasp, do not waste time by repeatedly reading the whole passage in the hope that the gist of it will eventually be understood. Instead proceed to the next stage.

(b) Divide the passage into sections which can be more easily retained in the mind when you come to look at the meaning in detail. Usually each paragraph can be treated on its own; otherwise separate the passage into suitable self-contained portions of about 100 words.

The above procedure needs to be adopted whichever method is to be followed hereafter.

METHOD A is suitable for passages which are predominantly factual.

Stage 1. Read through the first paragraph or section to see if any phrases or words can be omitted. Unnecessary repetition, illustrations of general points and other inessentials should be left out, thereby allowing the important facts to be seen more clearly.

At the same time, where possible substitute single words or short phrases for longer phrases at points where it will not entail actually altering the construction of the sentences.

To make these modifications clear before moving on to Stage 2, place square brackets round the material to be omitted; underline those phrases which are to be substituted and write above the alternative words. This not only assists in reducing the length of the passage but also replaces some of the original wording.

Stage 2. With the inessential matter removed and certain phrases already condensed, you are now faced with a task less formidable than it had at first appeared. The remaining material needs now to be summarized in the required number of words by rewriting. Take care to preserve the continuity of ideas especially between paragraphs.

In their reports, examiners frequently complain of faulty proportioning of the précis, where candidates have squandered words at one place, necessitating a drastic reduction of words somewhere else. If you keep each paragraph to the correct proportion of words allowed, this fault will not arise.

The technique outlined above needs then to be applied to the remaining sections of the passage.

By treating the précis in two stages, even the most difficult extract is made more manageable. Stage 1 can be completed for the whole passage in less than ten minutes, leaving the rest of the allocated time for Stage 2.

Sample Passage. Method A

At the end of the war [After the war] I [had had to] investigate [investigated] a minor outbreak of hashish smuggling from the Middle East, [but the profits here were not large,] and I had no real difficulty in stopping it. [easily stopped it.]

[The first hint I got that organized narcotics smuggling was beginning on our aircraft came in a roundabout way.] (see next paragraph) There had always been a certain amount [some] of watch-smuggling, involving certain crew members on [the Far Eastern] routes between Hongkong and Tokyo. [Watch prices in Tokyo were just that much higher than in Hongkong to make it worth people's while to take a dozen expensive watches in with them when they landed.] I knew this went on, but there are some things a security officer has to turn a blind eye to [ignore] particularly when he has only a limited staff. The amounts were not large, [small] it would have been difficult to prove, and I had more important things [work] [on my plate] at the time.

[But then,] early in 1954, a [disturbing] rumour reached me in London [that had me really worried.] [It was] from a [reliable] source in Hongkong [that had been unusually accurate in the past.] [According to what I heard,] the organization [we had always] suspected to be behind the watch traffic had started taking the movement out of the watches, filling the cases with heroin, and [then] giving them to [unsuspecting] crew members for delivery in Tokyo [without telling them what they were up to.]

This really made me furious, [and I did not see why a group of

79

smart gentlemen in Hongkong should be allowed to trick our people into carrying out their extremely dangerous dirty work for them][There is all the difference in the world between smuggling a watch and smuggling narcotics.] [It was] because I knew how strong the feeling was against drug-running within B.O.A.C. [that] I was able to stop this particular traffic [as] easily [as I did.]
(322 words.) *The Sunday Times.*

Précis

DRUG SMUGGLING ON B.O.A.C. AIRCRAFT

The writer stated that as a security officer he had easily stopped a minor outbreak of hashish smuggling from the Middle East. There had always been some watch-smuggling by crew members on routes between Hongkong and Tokyo. He had ignored this as the quantities were small, proof would have been difficult, and with a limited staff, he had more important work at the time. Early in 1954, a disturbing rumour reached him in London from a reliable source in Hongkong. The suspected organization was replacing the watch movements with heroin, giving the cases to unsuspecting crew members for delivery in Tokyo. This deception infuriated him. Because of the strong feeling against drug-running within B.O.A.C., he easily put an end to it.
(124 words.)

METHOD B is suitable for passages of a more literary character. Here direct repetition is more difficult to detect and the use of figurative language may obscure the underlying theme. For these reasons it is often unsatisfactory to apply Method A regarding the omission of superfluous wording although this may be adopted in parts of the précis.

Stage 1. Read through the first paragraph underlining what appear to be the main points; here you should concentrate more upon the ideas of the author than upon the actual wording or language he uses.

Stage 2. If the passage is uncomplicated write down in your own words and in sentence form the argument which the author is trying to convey. In the case of a more difficult extract, the rough draft may need to be at first in note form.

Even at this point, the approximate proportion of words for each paragraph must be maintained. This will save the time which many candidates waste by attempting to delete excessive wording, and often damaging the value of the précis as a result.

In this type of passage, there is a greater danger of incorporating words and phrases from the original which prove unsuitable in the context of your abbreviated rendering. The instruction of the examiners that candidates should avoid the wording of the original as far as possible is given not to make the question more difficult but because a more satisfactory result is always achieved by rewriting than by a manipulation of the original phraseology. It is almost impossible to maintain the subtle characteristics of style that distinguish a literary passage when you are allowed only one-third of the words. Fragments 'lifted' from the given extract will usually be incongruous in the midst of your simplified and condensed version.

Sample Passage. Method B

That faint, fairy-needle prickling at the back of the nose, the sensation that the body, waking from sleep, is a shade too warm around the chops, the merest hint too chilly on the extremities, arouse in combination the flicker of a suspicion that the Common Cold may have been caught yet again.

Lie still, cold-catcher. Fight! It's psychosomatic. It's all in the mind. Your luck, cold-catcher, cannot be running this low.

And here it is—a really splendid one, a champion right up there in the heavyweight division. That fairy-needle prickling never lies. Soon, now, the invading hordes of microbes—I once heard them described as Genghis Khold and his Catartar raiders—will possess the whole head and chest, bunging up ears, eyes, nose and lungs, reducing the very soul to a wet handkerchief.

How, you wish to know, does the experienced cold-catcher react to catching yet another cold, having had three beauties already since Christmas? What preventive or therapeutic measures does he take, in view of the fact that if this sort of thing goes on he must surely be heading for an early grave?

The experienced cold-catcher does nothing at all! No pill, no tablet, no cough-drop passes his burning lips. Nothing is spread on, sniffed up or gargled. Masterly inaction is the experienced cold-catcher's portion, for the solid and sufficient reason that no pill, no tablet, coughdrop or other medicament has ever been known to do him the slightest good. This negative action not only saves money but also hours of time that might otherwise be squandered upon pill swallowing, gargle mixing, kettle boiling, linctus swilling, to say nothing of the endless journeys backwards and forwards to the chemist, and certainly not to mention the greatest waste of all—waiting for these medicaments to make one feel a little better, before one's time.

There's a futile exercise, beneath the experienced catcher's contempt. He knows what happens when Genghis Khold and his Catartar raiders breach the fortifications. No power on earth can get them out until they've done their usual thorough job of looting, sacking and burning, and least of all a mere gargle or a tablespoon of lung tonic. Once the raiders get in they stay until they're good and ready to pack up and go and assault someone else, leaving of course a hacking cough behind as a reminder that they'll almost certainly be back in full force round about the week after next.

(420 words.)   Patrick Campbell, *Sunday Times.*

Précis
THE ALL-TOO-COMMON COLD

A tickling at the back of the nose and extremes of temperature within the body indicate that again you have caught a cold. At first you think it is imagination, but as the symptoms develop, your whole body becomes affected. How does the experienced cold-catcher react? He does nothing at all; he takes no cough-mixture or pills, thereby saving not only money but also time which might have been wasted waiting for the medicine to take effect. He knows there is no cure for the cold. Instead he waits for the germs to go of their own accord, knowing that they will certainly return the week after next.

(112 words.)

By following either of these methods and preserving a careful balance of the number of words for each paragraph, the finished précis should be approximately the number of words stipulated.

Examination reports draw attention to three faults of précis writing that are frequently criticized. These are:

(a) The final version does not make sense.
(b) Faulty proportioning.
(c) Too many phrases taken directly from the original passage.

Both methods illustrated above will enable you to avoid these errors.

General Hints

(a) The précis must be written as far as possible in your own words.

(b) If the instructions state that the passage must be condensed to not more than 130 words, you will be penalized if you exceed this figure by even one word. About 130 words may be considered to mean 120–140 words.

(c) Passages for summary written in the first person should be treated in reported speech, i.e., turned into the third person singular and the past tense where applicable. In this case the identity of the author and the context of the passage must be established at the beginning.

In his Autobiography, John Stuart Mill said that ...

If the passage is anonymous, 'The speaker stated that ...' is a suitable way to begin, but this phrase must be used only when the original is in direct speech.

(d) Vary the length of sentences; the number of sentences will be reduced in about the same proportion as the number of words.

(e) Avoid direct questions and figurative language which may have appeared in the original.

(f) Most illustrations and examples can be omitted or replaced by a collective term, unless they are vital to the passage.

(g) Do not waste time counting words until the whole précis is complete. One line of handwriting contains about eight words; this is sufficient as a guide to the number of words while the précis is being written.

If the passage is treated one paragraph at a time and the approximate proportion of words is maintained, then no serious exceeding of the stipulated number of words can arise. Count the words and give an accurate total at the end of the précis. Falsification of this figure will be quickly detected by the examiner who may deduct marks for dishonesty or poor arithmetic.

(h) The completed précis should be one paragraph, since usually it covers only one topic, unless there is a particular reason why the passage must be presented in more than one paragraph. A single paragraph makes the précis more compact in appearance and emphasizes the unity of the ideas it contains.

(i) Provide a suitable title whether or not it is asked for by the examiners. Do not be too general but choose a title which can apply to that particular extract only. The title does not count in the number of words.

(j) When the précis is complete, read it through and compare it with the original to see that no important facts have been omitted and that no meaning or emphasis has been altered.

(k) Check the spelling of words which might be wrong.

The purpose of summarizing correspondence

Often in an office it is necessary to summarize a letter or a series of letters. If a large firm retains in its files all the letters it has received and copies of all those despatched in reply, the quantity of correspondence can amount to tons of paper over a few years.

Where a sequence of letters covers a routine matter, a summary of the whole series can be contained on one sheet of paper, which can be kept in the files in place of perhaps the five or six sheets of paper of the original letters. In this way there is an economy of both space and money.

In some organizations which receive hundreds of letters each day, it is the duty of certain members of staff to précis the correspondence as soon as it arrives in the morning. The summaries are circulated to each department so that managers can request to see the original of any letter which might be their responsibility. This system avoids the time-wasting which results from passing a letter from one department to another until it reaches the appropriate person who should deal with it.

Preparation

The summary of correspondence presents a number of additional factors to those encountered in a normal summary.

(a) The précis requires a simple standard heading, e.g.
Summary of the correspondence between Mr. F. James, 6 Holly Lane, Ashtead, Surrey, and Messrs. Bradley and Tomkins, 16 Heath Road, Brentwood, Essex, concerning an order for a Bosworth bookcase.

(b) If the dates of a series of letters have no special significance, the first and last dates can be included in the heading after the second address, e.g., 'from 6th November to 15th November, 19—'. If the dates are important to the correspondence, they must be retained at the beginning of each letter summary. The heading does not count towards the total number of words. It must be set out clearly as a heading, and separated from the précis itself.

(c) All formal acknowledgements and complimentary phrases are omitted.

(d) Details of importance must not be generalized. All specifications, quantities, numbers, sizes, dates of delivery, and other facts relating to the purpose of the correspondence must appear in full.

(e) The summary of each letter should be set out as a separate paragraph so that the pattern of the correspondence is clear at a glance.

Sample summary correspondence

Give a clear summary in about 75 words of the following letters. Supply also a heading, in which names and addresses may be given.

Charles Fowler & Sons,
38 Castle Street,
Jarvis Mill,
Kent.
15th March, 19—.

Messrs. Stanley & Earl,
Newcastle-upon-Tyne.

Dear Sirs,

We recently ordered from you one Stokewell Ashfree Stove, which was subsequently delivered to our premises in Jarvis Mill either late evening or early morning when the shop was closed. The stove was left in our yard without a delivery note or signature.

When we discovered the stove, we sent it at once to our client, Mr. Jack Pipe, a plumber, in the packing in which it was received by us. When Mr. Pipe unpacked it he found that the top and two mica panels in the fire-door were broken.

We realize that a few days have elapsed since delivery but we hope you will be able to replace the broken parts.

Yours faithfully,
CHARLES FOWLER & SONS.

Stanley & Earl,
Newcastle-upon-Tyne.
18th March, 19—.

Messrs. Charles Fowler & Sons,
38 Castle Street,
Jarvis Mill,
Kent.

Dear Sirs,

We have received your letter of 15th March and note your remarks regarding the Stokewell Ashfree Stove which was delivered when your premises were closed.

We find it hard to believe that our lorry driver would do this as he is a most reliable man, but we will, of course, accept your statement and arrange to despatch the replacements free of charge towards the end of this week.

         Yours faithfully,
         STANLEY & EARL.

         Charles Fowler & Sons,
         38 Castle Street,
         Jarvis Mill,
         Kent.
         22nd March, 19—

Messrs. Stanley & Earl,
Newcastle-upon-Tyne.

Dear Sirs,
  We have today received one top for a Stokewell Ashfree Stove together with two fire-door mica panels in good condition.

We wish to point out, however, that we returned to you the fire-door as well as the top and the mica panels.

Will you please let us have the door as soon as possible?

    Yours faithfully,
    CHARLES FOWLER & SONS.

         Stanley & Earl,
         Newcastle-upon-Tyne.
         25th March, 19—

Messrs. Charles Fowler & Sons,
38 Castle Street,
Jarvis Mill,
Kent.

Dear Sirs,
  Thank you for your letter of 22nd March. We cannot understand the remarks in your second paragraph as we can find no mention in your last letter of the fire-door being returned. Moreover we have not received the door.

Would you kindly let us know whether the complete fire-door was returned or the right or left door only?

It is, of course, unnecessary to remove the fire-door in order to replace the mica, and as the fire-doors are fitted with great precision in our works, due care must be take to replace them correctly, or the working will be seriously affected.

Yours faithfully,
STANLEY & EARL.
Royal Society of Arts.

Précis

Summary of the correspondence between Charles Fowler & Sons, 38 Castle Street, Jarvis Mill, Kent, and Messrs. Stanley & Earl, of Newcastle-upon-Tyne, from 15th March to 25th March 19—, regarding a Stokewell Ashfree Stove.

Fowler & Sons complained that a Stokewell Ashfree Stove, delivered to their shop, had been left without a delivery note or signature. Also the top and two mica panels were broken.

Stanley & Earl expressed regret and agreed to send replacement parts free of charge.

Fowler & Sons acknowledged receipt of the replacements but said that the fire-door had not been returned.

Stanley & Earl denied receiving the door, pointing out that it was unnecessary to remove the door.

(81 words.)

EXERCISES

1. Summarize the following passage in about 100 words.

Automation on the assembly line is brought within reach of small as well as large manufacturers in Britain today with the introduction for the first time of a new low-cost industrial robot.

Designed to work on any assembly line under the command of its own electronic brain, it was demonstrated in London recently 5 by its creator, Mr. Edwin F. Shelley.

Known as the TransfeRobot 200, this versatile new device is now in production in the U.S.A. and is already being used by a number of large companies in the manufacture of such varied products as clocks, business machines, razors and automotive and electrical 10 equipment.

Mr. Shelley, vice-president of U.S. Industries, Inc., and creator of the TransfeRobot concept, introducing the machine said:

'It is capable of performing thousands of tasks in assembly and related operations, and is the first general-purpose automation 15 machine to be made available to manufacturers as standard off-the-shelf hardware.'

All previous products in this field, he said, have been special-purpose or custom-built machines. The cost of these was generally prohibitive for the smaller manufacturer—and larger organizations had also to expend very large capital sums to lay down production lines which it was extremely costly to switch from one job to another.

If manufacturers can get years of routine bench work done at the price of only roughly one year's wages, and the elimination of workers who hold up production because they are late, or to indulge in tea breaks, or to go-slow, or even to go on strike, they are obviously going to be extremely interested in Mr. Shelley's creation.

(271 words.) *The New Daily.*

2. Summarize the following extract in not more than 100 words.

Life in the 20th century is held together by paper. In all its forms, printed and unprinted, paper is encountered in every sphere of human activity, being handled or looked at, stored or treasured and consumed in a thousand different ways. It is one of those familiar things that is taken for granted. Its appearance as paper—its qualities and dimensions—are rarely seen consciously. Thus a controversy over paper sizes may seem remote from the ordinary consumer: 'What', he may ask, 'is it to do with me?' The answer is 'Quite a lot!' Superficially the arguments for and against Britain's adoption of International Paper Sizes as standard for stationery and the majority of other paper products may seem to belong to the same category as arguments over decimal currency, metric measurement and so on. The difference lies in the gradual nature of the change to IPS. If, eventually, IPS becomes the standard in Britain it will do so by degrees. A start has already been made and IPS has received the blessing of influential organizations of many kinds: the British Standards Institution is for IPS, so is the British Federation of Master Printers, the Society of Industrial Artists, the Royal Institute of British Architects and the National Federation of Builders' and Plumbers' Merchants. Many firms, large and small, have adopted IPS for either the whole or a part of their stationery requirements. Amongst the largest are Imperial Chemical Industries, the British Motor Corporation, GEC and Shell International. The lead offered by these giants has been followed for convenience by many firms who work closely with them, and there are others who have decided for themselves in favour of IPS.

(282 words.) *Paper at Work*, No. 4, Spicers Ltd.

3. Summarize the following extract in not more than 130 words.

Enlightened firms nowadays look upon business stationery as one of the most important single items in helping to create a good impression of their company to the world outside. Good quality paper, good design and good printing are the first essentials. But they are only a beginning—stars waiting in the wings. Before a firm's 5 stationery is ready to play its part in public, a fourth ingredient must be added—the typing.

In many ways the typist's contribution is a decisive one. But it is by no means the easiest because much more is required than an accurate transcription of what has been dictated or written. Working against 10 time and with varying subject-matter, today's typist must also be, in part, a designer. Her work determines the quality of the whole presentation. How, then, can a firm try to ensure consistently good 'typing in style' all through its various departments? One effective way is to give guidance to the typists—to establish a style of the house 15 that is based on sound principles. The job this Guide sets out to do is to provide the businessman, and his typists, with an outline of these principles.

Although good style is the aim, it is not the only—or even the first —thing to be considered. The function of typed documents is not 20 simply to impress people by their looks; it is to convey information in the clearest and most readable form. The pursuit of style to the neglect of clearness and readability would defeat the document's purpose.

Fortunately, however, no choice is called for. True style is the 25 result, not the rival, of clearness and legibility. At least where letters and reports are concerned, the document arranged for easy reading is always the best-looking, and the best-looking always the easiest to read. This complete integration of function and style—of the art of the designer and the skill of the typist—automatically follows when 30 a few simple rules are observed. These rules are not inflexible. They can be freely adapted in any that personal taste dictates. Use them to make your typed documents convey information in the most readable way, and style will inevitably result.

(390 words.)   *Paper at Work*, No. 3, Spicers Ltd.

4. Summarize the following passage in about 140 words.

One may risk the conclusion, even without the benefit of extensive research, that standards of driving will be better, disregard of the

89

law less frequent, and accidents fewer where the roads are thick with mobile police patrols than where patrolling is weak. The interest of the Automobile Association's survey of the practice in foreign countries is not so much in its confirmation of this obvious assertion as in the picture it gives of how patrolling is organized elsewhere. Undermanning is almost everywhere the limiting factor in the effectiveness of this means of enforcement. Staffing is also at the heart of the further question, which is much debated, whether mobile traffic duty should be done as part of ordinary police duties, or by a special organization within the police forces, or by a separate corps of traffic police with no wider duties. The first and second of these are the methods commonly employed abroad, the third hardly at all.

Yet a separate traffic corps is not without its advocates in Britain, among which is now the Law Society. The proposal is in line with its other idea that minor traffic offences should be disentangled from the apparatus of the criminal law and dealt with under different procedures. Minor infringements of the traffic code would then fall under a separate system of justice, while enforcement of the code along with other traffic duties would pass from the police to a separately formed body. This, it is held, apart from any other advantages would greatly ease the man-power problems of the police by relieving them of the innumerable hours spent on traffic duty and consequentially in court, and enabling them to concentrate more of their resources on crime prevention and detection. Perhaps; but the recruitment problem would crop up again in the context of new traffic corps. The new corps might drain recruits from the police. It is also questionable whether a line drawn between criminality and motoring offences and between general law enforcement and traffic law enforcement is as clear or convenient as it may appear at first sight. One would have to be satisfied that the police could be divested of traffic duties without any loss of opportunity to perform their other duties successfully and without any duplication with the new traffic corps.

(387 words.)
The Times.

5. Summarize the following passage in about 150 words.

Each proposal for a new university is a dagger pointing at the heart of the golf clubs. And well they know it, those shrewd, jolly men from the banks and the insurance offices. They are accustomed to look death in the face—nothing yellow about any of them when they fought the Hun—and they won't go down now without a fight. But what can they do against those smart fellows at the U.G.C. ?* The plan to take away their golf course, hatched with some bounder from the county council, is bound to go through in the end. Look at the way, they tell themselves glumly, poor old Norwich was sold down the river. The very idea of destroying a golf course to put up a university! And so they drink up, and try that dicey short hole by the stream once more, and do it in bogey, only to be bunkered at the long fourteenth by the water-tank.

It is tragic, of course, to think of the golf clubs being closed down all over the country. But nothing—not even the cultural traditions of the golf club—must be allowed to stand in the way of our university expansion programme. Those green, smiling oases, which the golf clubs nobly preserved from speculative builders, must now play a still more vital role in our economy. Picture the pile-driver on that elevated third tee, from where a full shot with a brassie could break a window in the club house. Bull-dozers will lumber along the fairways, and excavators devour the greens. It is sad, and yet exhilarating. In a couple of years a senior common room will stand on the site of the club house. Then it will be port, instead of gin and tonic, that circulates round the table. And instead of the artless conversation of golfers you will hear the marvellous erudition of dons.

'You can expel nature with a pitch-fork, but it will always return.' Horace may be right. Will the ghosts of departed golfers still walk the long fairways and stand reverently by the greens? Will Dog-Leg Hall (as the first new hall of residence will be called) echo to the eerie cry of 'Fore'? The dons, at any rate, will exult in the creation of a new sort of Redbrick. Instead of gowns, the academic body will wear Fair Isle sweaters. Spiked shoes will be compulsory at lectures. And, after raising £5m. by public subscription, the new university will build a brand-new golf course on its site.

(430 words.) *Times Educational Supplement.*

6. Summarize the following passage in about 150 words.

The problem of drug dependence can affect any social class and no family or group is immune from the risk or the tragedies that can occur.

It has been said that three factors combine to make people dependent on drugs. There must be a basic personality weakness,

* University Grants Committee.

either inherited or acquired in some way. This personality must experience a crisis of some sort; and at that moment the drug must be available.

Most unstable young people, if given a healthy social atmosphere, will steer their way through adolescence and ultimately become reasonably stable adults. But if drugs are easily available, then drug taking becomes fashionable. People who would normally never dream of taking pills, unless prescribed for them by a doctor, will submit to social pressure and try them or *pretend* to have tried them in order to follow the trend. This creates a climate of acceptance and tempts those who are psychologically unstable to experiment with drugs. They may come to depend on them as artificial props at the very time that they should be developing independence and self reliance. It is not surprising that drug-taking is often described as a contagious or socially infectious disease. Some have gone as far as to call it an epidemic. 'The problem lies not in the drug but in the taker.'

He or she may see an exaggerated newspaper advertisement for some mild pep pill and come to believe in it so much that the advertised pill temporarily boosts his confidence (PLACEBO EFFECT). Even though it is fairly harmless in itself, it creates a habit and desire for stimulation which it cannot satisfy.

The first encounter with pep pills containing AMPHETAMINE, a stimulant, is usually at coffee bars, clubs, parties or dances, where he may also be introduced to 'reefer' cigarettes containing the drug CANNABIS ('marijuana', 'pot', etc.). Pills and cannabis have a host of nicknames. Once the pills have produced artificial elation and confidence, he will want more. Tolerance develops quickly. The initial one or two pills or tablets in an evening may become ten or twenty at a time, and they no longer satisfy him. He knows that this pill taking is illegal but he needs these pills and since the practice is tolerated amongst his friends, his respect for the law and police is weakened.

(409 words.) *Drug Dependence*, Dr. Antony J. Wood
(Medico-Social Publications).

7. Summarize the following passage in about 150 words.

Nothing stamps its mark on a man so much as his baggage. Our earliest recognition of status came from the way our schoolmates regarded our satchel. An indeterminate brown cloth, with mottled green piping at the edges, and a tattered pair of leather

straps: this was the measure of us in the eyes of the class. It was 5
years before we were able to overcome the deplorable image that
satchel gave us. A pair of school colours and a bronze medal in the
high jump finally did the trick. But so much heart-throb and per-
secution would have been avoided if we had only known that the
satchel was dead as the dodo and boys should carry a suitcase. 10

It was the same when we took our first job. The suitcase we
carried proudly to the office was seized on as a convenient symbol
of our refusal to conform. Conform? Nothing we should have liked
better. But how could we have guessed that suitcases were considered
eccentric in our chambers? A brief-case was the key to conformity, 15
even a Gladstone bag sufficed to show that you were an intellectual.
But a suitcase: no, this was unthinkable in those Dickensian precincts. Eagerly we acquired a shiny new brief-case from the Civil
Service Stores across the road. The juniors' laughter went up an
octave. A *new* brief-case? Why, no one had ever had a new brief- 20
case in those chambers. One inherited the things, like a decently
tattered gown at Christ Church. It was no good making any bones
about us: we looked like a businessman up for the day from Bir-
mingham.

The taunts took effect. We left the law and plunged into business. 25
Our now battered brief-case achieved a pleasant anonymity among
the tidal streams of commuters ebbing and flowing in the City
each day. Not that the really smart businessmen seemed to carry a
case at all. They passed smiling past the barrier at Cannon Street
and were snatched up by discreet black saloons from their offices. 30
No doubt despatch riders had already collected and deposited their
papers. Often a secret file would leave our office during the afternoon destined for some tycoon to read that night in his villa on the
heights of Box Hill or in the green valley of the Thames. And sometimes in the heat of the day another no less secret file would arrive 35
from a different tycoon in his wooded lair near Woking.

Yes, the secret of status was to carry no luggage at all. We tried
it with miraculous success. Oddly enough it made no difference to
our work that we carried no luggage to the office. For, truth to
tell, it had always been an empty symbol. 40

(461 words.) *Times Educational Supplement.*

8. At the Annual General Meeting of Amalgamated Processes
Ltd., the Chairman delivered the Annual Report. Make a summary
of the Report in about 140–150 words and supply a suitable heading.

In presenting the Balance Sheet for the year 19— your directors are pleased to be able to report for the second year in succession a marked increase in the net profits and a general improvement in turnover and they are the more pleased to be able to do so as this has resulted from their steady pursuance of the policy of maintaining equipment at the very highest level of efficiency and replacing at the earliest possible moment all equipment the continuing efficiency of which they had any cause to doubt. An examination of the Balance Sheet before you will show that the figures for maintenance and replacement are high. That your directors admit, but they submit to you that there is no cause for alarm or despondency, since these figures are balanced by others, even higher than usual, on the other side.

You are aware, of course, that overseas trading is still very difficult. Many of our former markets, for reasons with which you are all only too painfully familiar, remain almost or wholly closed to us. Nevertheless I feel that this state of affairs need cause no undue concern. There are already signs—at the moment too slight to be termed more than fairly encouraging—which can be interpreted by those in close contact with the general trend of trade as at least not discouraging, and you may rest assured that your directors are not neglecting any opportunity to take advantage of every opening that can be discerned. As and when such openings present themselves they will be seized without any delay.

Meanwhile every advantage has been taken of the increasing opportunities in the home market. Our business in this country has been 60 per cent of our total business during the whole of the year, an increase of 8 per cent on last year's figures. No slackening of effort will be allowed to hamper our success in this market for the ensuing twelve months.

Your directors recommend a dividend of 12 per cent as against the previous dividend of 10 per cent and they feel that this will in no way impair the Company's resources.

He would be a bold man who in these difficult days would hazard a detailed prophecy as to the future but I feel justified in predicting no great drop in our turnover. Your directors keep ever in mind the problem before them and I think you may indulge in at least a modest hope of business being better still next year.

The Report and Balance Sheet were then adopted.

(427 words.)   *Royal Society of Arts.*

9. Summarize the following passage in not more than 150 words.

Ever since the Trust first acquired properties, seventy-five years ago, it has had to contend with the litter problem. As its responsibilities have grown so has the task of coping with the untidiness left behind by visitors, with the deliberate dumping of rubbish on Trust land and with the unsightly nuisance of paper blowing in from else- 5 where. The problem has been tackled in a number of ways. At some places the Trust employs wardens, one of whose tasks is litter collection. At other properties this work is done voluntarily, and a recent development at Ashridge might be followed at other places. Local residents there have formed themselves into a group of vigilantes. 10 Each member accepts responsibility for a part of the property. Their task is to collect litter and also to educate visitors to take their litter home.

At some properties the Trust finds that litter bins, far from easing the problem can aggravate it. At these the aim is to create an atmo- 15 sphere in which it becomes unthinkable to drop litter. This can be helped by 'take your litter home' notices. At others, and particularly where there are restaurants and snack bars, litter bins are needed; here it is essential to arrange that the local authority has frequent collections of rubbish. The Trust is represented on the Council of 20 the Keep Britain Tidy Group and in this and in other ways it does its best within its resources to preserve its properties and the countryside as a whole from being spoiled.

It seems to the Council that in recent years this problem has become a more urgent one. Wherever one drives along country roads there are 25 now too frequently places where litter is much worse than it was a short time ago. To some extent this is due to the use of new and more durable packaging materials, particularly plastics, for substances varying from fertilizers to sweets, and it indicates that countrymen are often as much to blame as townspeople. The main cause however 30 seems to be an increasing apathy on the part of the public as a whole. Bodies like the National Trust can play a part and must continue to do so. So too can individuals, and there is great scope in this for members of the Trust. The problem however is a national one and it can only be tackled nationally by a centrally directed and expensive 35 campaign of education and by continuing vigorous action on the part of the local authorities. Stricter enforcement of the existing law seems to the Council to be necessary.

(445 words.) *The National Trust Report 1968–69.*

10. Summarize the following passage in about 160 words.

LONDON FISH AND FOOD SUPPLY

This afternoon the inquiry instituted by the Corporation into the fish and food supply of the metropolis was resumed at the Guildhall, Mr. W. H. Pannell in the chair. Mr. Cholmondley Fennell stated that he was the Government Inspector of fisheries from 1866 to
5 1874. He had visited France, Scotland, Ireland and various parts of England in his official capacity, and was well acquainted with the fishing industry. He was clearly of the opinion that unless there was legislation on the subject, soles and oysters on the British coasts would become extremely scarce. He knew from personal observation
10 that the price of fish in Paris was fifty per cent less than in London; but he was unable to give any satisfactory reason for the difference, notwithstanding that London was so much nearer the sea than Paris. He suggested that a new market should be opened, as Billingsgate was not capable of supplying the wants of London. It was
15 perfectly impossible that it could be the centre for the Metropolitan Fish Supply. He suggested that, without abolishing Billingsgate, other markets should be opened close to the large railway termini of those lines which conveyed the greatest proportion of fish to London. This, he thought, was the most practical suggestion. Water
20 carriage was slow, whereas the railway was fast. He was of the opinion that, if these markets were established, a very large supply of fish could be supplied and carried at half the present rate. He had purchased fish at Plymouth for 1s. 4d. which he knew he would have to pay 8s. for if he bought it retail in Bond Street. The principal
25 cause of this was the monopoly which existed. He was aware that the excessive charges were owing, in a great measure, to the profits which some fishmongers stood out for. Mr. A. Macpherson, belonging to a firm of fish salesmen, Billingsgate, said he desired to contradict an important but inaccurate statement made by one of his servants
30 towards the close of the proceedings yesterday afternoon. The statement complained of was to the effect that the salesmen charged the senders in one instance £4 12s. for the porterage of 183 packages, which were carried into the market for 5s. The fact really was that although this man might have received 5s., he and other porters
35 were engaged at regular weekly wages; and there was in addition the salaries of the clerks, cost of warehousing, and the railway carriage when returning empties, all of which charges had to come out of the £4 12s. and fully swallowed up the whole amount. This clearly proved, that instead of the salesmen having a profit on the

96

empties, it was a decided loss. Witness, at the chairman's request, 40 agreed to supply the Committee with railway receipts and other documents, in order to prove his statement. The inquiry was again adjourned.
(486 words.) *London Evening News*, 26th July, 1881.

11. Summarize the following extract in about 130 words.

By far the most important piece of advice for anyone wishing to write for radio and television is to listen and view as much as possible. B.B.C. radio does not exist to cater for those with a vague feeling that they would like to talk on the air, and B.B.C. television was not created to provide a home for plays which have found no place on 5 the West End stage. Radio and television are distinctive means of communication with their own limitations and possibilities and their own particular techniques, and anyone who seriously wishes to sell his work to the B.B.C. must first make himself familiar with its existing output. 10

Second, like every other type of freelance writing, the potential scriptwriter must study his market. There is, for instance, no single type of radio play, for the B.B.C.'s large output is broken down into distinctive series, each with their own characteristics. A play will have a far better chance of acceptance if the writer decides in the 15 beginning whether he is, say, writing for a Third Programme audience or a Light Programme one, and even more if he has in mind a specific series such as 'Saturday Night Theatre' or 'The Monday Night Play'.

The same is true of talks. It is not sufficient to decide that one would like to deliver a talk on one's recent holiday. Instead the would-be 20 author must ask himself: 'What Programme is most likely to use material of this sort?'; 'Is there a particular series within that Programme into which it might fit?'; 'Have they used similar, but not too similar, items before?'; and, not least important, 'What length of talk do they prefer?' Similar rules apply to television. 25

The television audience has been studied in great detail, and a television programme is likely to be produced with a particular 'slot' in mind, that is a particular time on a particular day of the week. The audience at 7 p.m. on Friday is different from the 9 p.m. audience on Saturday, and both are different from the 5 p.m. audience on 30 Sunday. The author must not be hypnotized by the varying requirements of particular audiences, but they will certainly be in the mind of the producers and executives who ultimately decide whether or not to buy his work.
(407 words.) *Writing for the B.B.C.* (B.B.C. Publications).

12. Summarize the following passage in about 180 words.

BLACKWOOD, MORTON & SONS LTD.

The increase in turnover on the high figure already reached in 19— is an indication of the success both of the Company's sales organization and of our designers in anticipating public taste. World sales in 19— to customers outside the Group exceeded £10½ million
5 and, for the third year in succession, the Company has increased its share of woven carpet sales by U.K. manufacturers.

For a number of reasons, the improvement in turnover is not fully reflected in the profit for the year. Adverse factors included labour costs, which increased as a result of higher wage rates and
10 the introduction of a shorter working week in March; the necessity to write down stocks of wool and other raw materials; higher interest rates and overheads; and a less favourable result from the Canadian subsidiary. In addition, the sustained increase in demand outran the capacity of our own spinning mills and necessitated the purchase
15 of pile yarn from outside sources.

Once again, we have been successful in expanding our exports, and have obtained particularly good results from Australia, West Germany, and Denmark. Our overseas promotion included participation in an exhibition in Frankfurt and in the exhibition at
20 Stockholm organized by the British Carpet Industry.

It is not sufficiently realized that many companies which are most active in supporting the country's drive for exports have to pay a penalty in terms of reduced productivity. In selling even to some of the best of our overseas markets, we have to compete for orders
25 which are only marginally profitable; locally based producers concentrate their efforts on the best-selling lines, and orders available **for British manufacturers are mainly for limited quantities and for designs which are seldom those most in demand in the U.K.**

In the present circumstances, it is undoubtedly in the national
30 interest for manufacturers to accept this penalty and we have had no hesitation in vigorously pursuing export sales and providing the designs and qualities that can be sold overseas. We should not, however, disguise the fact that our success in this field has added to the problems of those responsible for planning production and
35 maintaining the level of productivity.

Additional looms were brought into operation and more are due to be installed in the current year. New plant is also being installed to increase spinning capacity and to ensure as far as possible the supply of pile yarns from sources inside the Group.
40 As regards the current year, we should derive some benefit from

lower raw material costs—wool prices are lower than at this time last year and, with more concerns now engaged in nylon production in the U.K., we can anticipate a reduction in the price of nylon staple fibre—and this would be an offset against the continuing increases in other costs. If our overall costs of production continue 45 to rise, we can only maintain the present rate of profitability by expanding our turnover still further and in this the limiting factor will be the labour shortage. The Company has made strenuous efforts to recruit and train suitable labour and to make the best possible use of existing resources by the installation of fully up-to-date 50 plant. Our new ranges have been well received by retailers and sales to date this year are ahead of the level attained at this time last year. There have recently been signs of demand slackening as the result of credit limitations, but it is still too early to predict the long-term effect of the national economic situation on the consumer demand 55 for carpets.

(554 words.)

13. Summarize the following passage in about 230 words.

COMPANY MEETING—MANCHESTER LINERS LIMITED

The Sixty-seventh Annual General Meeting of Manchester Liners Limited was held at the registered office of the Company, St. Ann's Square, Manchester, on September 24th, 19—.

CHAIRMAN'S REPORT

It is satisfactory to be able to report that there was an improvement in trading conditions during the year under review, with cargo moving in greater volume. Unfortunately, in line with common experience, our costs continued to rise and the liner companies were compelled to increase their rates, an increase which was long 5 overdue.

Almost without exception every item which goes to make up our operating costs shows mounting increases, but one item in particular causes us the greatest concern. I refer, of course, to the delay experienced by our vessels in port and I say 'of course' because you 10 who have an interest in shipping will have read a great deal about this in the press in recent months and will appreciate the damaging effect these delays can have on voyage results.

You may ask is anything being done about it, or can anything be done about it. Confining ourselves to Manchester, our terminal 15 port, let me assure you that we work in the closest collaboration

99

with the Port Authority and it would not be too much to say that all the officials do their best to help us. Apart from the introduction of the 40-hour week for dock labour, which of itself was a sufficiently
20 restrictive handicap, they have been having an almost continuous shortage of labour and, whilst the Dock Labour Board has spread its net far and wide, suitable recruits have not been available in this area of full employment.

As always, our fleet has been maintained in the highest state of
25 efficiency. The 'Manchester Port', having served us well for many years has been sold for breaking up and her place taken by the new 'Manchester City', which vessel was partly financed through the Government Ship-building Credit Scheme. We have been encouraged by the competitive efficiency of the three new vessels on our Great
30 Lakes service and we have felt justified in ordering another 12,000 dead weight ton vessel from Smith's Dock Company, Middlesbrough, for delivery in April 19—. The purchase of these ships puts pressure on our capital resources, but the modernization and the resultant competitiveness of the fleet should justify this outlay.

35 Additionally, we have chartered two more vessels on a long-term basis and renamed them 'Manchester Freighter' and 'Manchester Engineer'; they are included in the list of the fleet at the end of this report. We have also been compelled to operate a further three vessels on short-term charter in order to offer the type of regular
40 service which merits support from both exporters and importers, and which is the very basis of our success. So here we have a paradox. On the one hand, we purchased modern vessels, which, by virtue of their greater service speed and advanced mechanical handling aids, should save tonnage, and on the other hand, we must charter
45 additional tonnage to fill the gaps caused by delays in port. Needless to say, this all costs money and will be reflected in our results.

I have made no reference to future prospects. This is difficult at any time, but even more difficult when the country faces such a grim outlook. I may appear to simplify too much when I say that
50 the main cause of our difficulties has been excessive national expenditure. A start has been made to cut this down, but whether enough remains to be seen.

I am sure shareholders would not wish me to omit from this review of the Company's affairs my usual tribute to the staff, ashore
55 and afloat, for their zealous and untiring work during a year in which there have been many difficulties and frustrations; they have tackled all problems readily, with satisfaction to the Company and themselves, and we tender to them our thanks and appreciation.

The report and accounts were adopted.

(644 words.)

14. Summarize the following passage in about 260 words.

When, because of accidents in fog, a motorway has to be closed and traffic diverted to the old road that the motorway is supposed to have replaced, every driver ought to put in some hard self-questioning. Why is British driving behaviour in fog collectively so lamentable? 5

Motorways ought to be reasonably safe in fog. They are not as safe as they could be made because successive Governments have been frightened by the cost of lighting them, and they remain unlit. But they are the best roads in Britain, one-way carriageways with no cross traffic, and even in dense fog they ought to be capable of 10 carrying cautious traffic safely. Instead, to drive on a motorway in fog is a terrifying experience—so terrifying that many drivers who are compelled to travel in fog deliberately choose routes that are far less good in order to avoid a motorway. Yet if it is possible to drive at all on an unimproved main road, it ought to be a great 15 deal easier to drive on a motorway. The peril is simply that motorway driving in bad conditions tends to be too fast for safety. The majority of drivers on a motorway in fog break the first rule of all driving— in any emergency they cannot stop within their range of vision. This is the fact behind those dreadful multiple crashes that occur 20 on motorways in fog; every car or lorry that runs into the wreckage of a crash in front of it does so because its driver is driving too fast to be able to stop in time. This is not bad luck; it is bad and dangerous driving.

Most of us following another car in fog have felt the psychological 25 temptation that we ourselves could do better than the man in front of us. Fog-vision, of course, varies, and some eyes are better than other, but all driving eyes, however good, share the same difficulty of peering into fog through a glass screen, and looking at myriads of water-droplets, each turned into a reflecting mirror 30 by the light that one needs to drive by. These common difficulties outweigh minor variations in individual eyesight. It is much easier to follow the red rear lights of a leading car in fog than to lead the column, and after a mile or two of driving behind someone else it is understandable to feel that one could do better on one's own. 35

No doubt it is possible for an experienced man to go faster in fog than an inexperienced driver, but unless the man in front stops and gives up, it is cruelty to push past him.

If the man in front can keep going, be patient and leave him to it, thanking your luck that you have someone to follow. But, remember, although his eyes are helping you, they are not replacing yours, and the fact that you are following him does not reduce by an iota your own driving responsibility.

Fog is always a more serious hazard at night than it is by day, but many recent accidents in fog have occurred in daylight—mostly around 8 to 9 a.m., when people are driving to work. A common cause—or contributory cause—of such accidents is the reluctance of British motorists to use headlamps by day. It has been well observed that British drivers tend to use lights 'as if the electricity were metered to them'. Sidelights are often all but invisible in daytime fog—next time you drive in daytime fog, keep a special watch for oncoming vehicles with sidelights only, and note how often you can see the vehicle itself before you can tell whether it has sidelights on or not. If you are driving on sidelights only, you will realize at once that your sidelights are no help at all to other traffic—indeed, they may be dangerous, because they give you a false sense of security. Whenever fog or mist by day calls for lights at all, dipped headlamps should be used. The test of whether lights are needed is simple—look at oncoming vehicles, and if you think that you would see them sooner if they carried lights—or saw them sooner because they carried lights—then your own lights are required. Lights are as necessary in daytime fog on motorways as on any other roads. There is not the same risk of meeting oncoming traffic, but it is just as important to carry rear lights, and dipped headlamps help vision slightly, and are valuable—perhaps lifesaving—to anyone who may be in the carriageway ahead after a breakdown or accident.

Fog accidents could be reduced from this week if all drivers would follow three rules. They are:

1. Never drive beyond the stopping limit of vision—even if it means crawling in bottom gear.
2. Use dipped headlights.
3. Be considerate—again, even if it means crawling in low gear for miles.

(834 words.) *The Guardian.*

15. Read the following passage, which contains about 500 words, and then write a summary of it in about 130 words. Your summary

should be in continuous prose and should avoid the use of the original wording of the passage.

Britain is the most urban nation in the world. Something like eighty per cent of us live in urban areas. In the last twenty years we have added over four million houses to our towns. And yet, considered either as architectural compositions or as utilities for the collective living of any reasonable kind of social life, our towns fall miserably short of what they should be. Our towns have been repulsive and inefficient for a hundred years and more—for so long, in fact, that most of us have become inured to their badness. Even those of us who are still aware of the possibility of a town's being an orderly, perhaps a beautiful, creation have come to regard the building of fine towns as a faculty which has somehow been denied to Englishmen.

Yet that is quite untrue. The English once built towns which, according to the standards of their times, were excellent instruments for the living of a good social life; which were altogether admirable essays in large-scale architectural composition. Those towns were at least as fine as any in their contemporary world. Incredible as it may seem now, they even held promise of our becoming the best of town-builders instead of what we have become: pretty nearly the worst.

Right up to a hundred years ago there was a remarkably strong and virile town tradition in England. That tradition was very different from the Continental tradition. It was none the worse for that. But it is a curious thing that today not only the ordinary citizen, but our professional men whose job it is to study and build towns, our architects and town-planners, are mostly unaware that such a tradition ever existed, and are content to belaud foreign towns and sigh plaintively because we have never built in precisely the same way in England.

Towns have sometimes been described as the physical expression of a nation's civilization. The physical form of a town does in many ways reflect fairly accurately the social condition of the people who live in it, their mode of life, their cultural achievement, their economic status, the kind of government they possess. The town reflects these characteristics because it arises out of them. It is, of course, precisely because of this that the English town tradition developed on its own individual lines.

Our fall from grace has been very deep during the last century. We are not very sensible, however, if because of that we forget that we once did, in fact, live and build in grace. It is, indeed, all the

40 more necessary for us to remember. The English contribution to the art of building towns was once an original and a valuable one. It is important that this should be realized, for if we are ever again to build good towns we shall need to restore our lost confidence, and perhaps to re-establish something of the old tradition.

These questions are based on the above passage.
(1) Explain what each of the following words means in its context in the passage. Use either a single word, or as short a phrase as possible, for each explanation.
repulsive (line 6)   inured (line 8)   faculty (line 11)
belaud (line 26)   mode (line 32).
(2) What does the writer mean when he describes towns as 'utilities for the collective living of any reasonable kind of social life'?
(3) Explain in your own words the meaning of the sentence, 'Our fall from grace has been very deep during the last century' (line 37).

Local Government Examinations Board

16. Read the following passage, which contains about 500 words, and then write a summary of it in about 130 words. Your summary should be in continuous prose and should avoid the use of the original wording of the passage.

It is reasonable to suppose that available leisure will continue to increase. But what will people do with it? Those who are so fortunate as to have a definite leaning towards music or the arts will have no problem, nor will those with strong intellectual tastes, for
5 whom the 'world is so full of a number of things' and who retain to maturity the fresh interest of childhood. But these people are now a minority of the population as a whole, and if one blames this on bad education they seem still in a minority though perhaps not a small one, among those well, or at least expensively, educated. If,
10 as I fear, it is more a matter of nature than of training, there will be many who will not wish to occupy their leisure in these ways. Will these be condemned to divide their time between super-television, the cinema and the football match? In this country, at least, gardening has a very wide appeal. A substantial fraction of the population,
15 perhaps even a majority of the male population, can happily spend quite a lot of time each week on a garden patch. Another group, smaller but still large, enjoys some mechanical hobby from household repairs to model railways.

The biggest unsatisfied demand is for adventure, which in Britain is expensive enough to be almost reserved for the professional and upper classes. This is the price we pay for a dense population, for most adventure needs space. It is dangerous to repress this desire or make it difficult to satisfy. Wars are caused, more than is generally admitted, by boredom, by the desire, unexpressed but for that reason all the stronger, to escape from a dull routine into exciting adventure. One of the advantages of being able to make food in factories is that it will release large areas of the world as playgrounds where men can follow for a time the traditional life of the hunter and fisher and regain touch with reality.

But this is not the only possible kind of adventure. I believe that space-travel will come fairly soon, and if so it will provide an outlet for communal effort like climbing Mount Everest, but on an enormously larger scale both as regards the number of people concerned and the time the effort will last. It will give young men the feeling, that they are engaged on something unique, worthy of all their efforts demanding self-sacrifice and calling to danger, bringing out to the full the joy of fellowship in a cause.

Answer the following questions which are based on the above passage.
(1) For each of the following words give another word which could be used in its place in the passage without altering the meaning:
retain (line 5)   occupy (line 11)   condemned (line 12)
substantial (line 14)   expensive (line 20)   desire (line 22)
release (line 27)   touch (line 29).
(2) Explain in your own words the meaning of the statement 'Those who are so fortunate as to have a definite leaning towards music or the arts will have no problem' (lines 2, 3 and 4).
(3) Why is adventure in Britain said to be expensive?

Local Government Examinations Board

17. Read the following passage, which contains about 550 words, and then write a summary of it in about 160 words.

The popular notion of the scientist as a recluse who makes great discoveries in the solitude of his laboratory was, in bygone days, sometimes true of the pure scientist. It is rarely so now. And it has never been true of the engineer. He can accomplish little except in co-operation with others. His day is crowded with talks, conferences, committees. His contacts with people are numerous and varied. In all of them mind addresses mind. It does so, sometimes through the spoken, sometimes through the written word. Talk and paper are, in these days, among the engineer's most important tools. He must learn to handle them well. The executive engineer has a greater use for them than for the tools that are found in the carpenter's and fitter's shops. So why think that these alone are educative? Why train engineers in the use of tools that they may never have to touch again once they have been launched on their professional career and teach them nothing about the tools that they *will* have to use?

The bad expositor may, and often does, provide an impressive volume of published work. It may contain a valuable record of profound thinking. But yet it will fail to be very effective. With sublime conceit he thinks himself, perhaps, superior to the obligations of mere craftsmanship; or it has never occurred to him that rather hard work has to be done whenever thought is being transferred from mind to mind; or, if it has occurred to him, he is content to let the reader do the whole of his work, to put into the right order in his mind what is in the wrong order on the paper, to draw the conclusions he is meant to even when they are not stated, to jump without guidance to the significance of a statement, to bridge any gap the author's carelessness may have left in a line of reasoning. The books of such an author are like quarries rich in previous ore hard to work. 'Let those who want the ore', the author seems to say, 'dig for it.' But will they? Need they?

Sometimes they have no choice. An author with unique and indispensable information has his readers at his mercy. The student who can find no well written textbook must use a badly written one. He must quarry hard in it if he would pass his examinations. Every expert, again, who would know what his contemporaries are doing, must spend many weary hours quarrying in atrociously composed contributions to learned societies. For well composed ones are all too rare. And the works manager who relies on his technical experts for guidance has often no choice but to take their reports home with him to read at leisure during long evenings. For he finds it useless to ask for verbal explanations; the spoken words of the experts prove no more illuminating than the written ones. So while he should be recuperating for the next day's task he must quarry instead; quarry among a disordered sequence of ideas, clumsy sentences, unfinished arguments, unexplained conclusions, undefined terms, ambiguous phrases. All of them, the undergraduate, the expert, the works manager, are turned into quarry slaves. The bad expositor is their master.

Professor R. Kapp, *Presentation of Technical Information.*

(1) Give briefly the meaning of the following words as they are used in the passage:
recluse (line 1)   expositor (line 16)   unique (line 31)
contemporaries (line 35)   learned societies (line 37)
recuperating (line 43).
(2) Why has the engineer never been a recluse?
(3) What tools does the executive engineer need to be able to use?
(4) In what respect will the bad expositor's book fail to be effective?
(5) Explain in your own words the sentence 'With sublime conceit he thinks himself, perhaps, superior to the obligations of mere craftsmanship (lines 18–20).

18. Read the following passage, which contains about 500 words, and then write a summary of it in about 130 words. Your summary should be written in continuous prose and should avoid the use of the original wording of the passage.

It is widely recognized that we must automate our industry or else we shall find ourselves unable to compete. But the technical changes in the field of automation are so rapid that it is difficult for anyone not directly involved to understand them and what they imply. One cannot reasonably expect the average Member of   5
Parliament, mainly concerned as he is bound to be with the many day-to-day problems of his constituency, to go much more deeply into the subject than to examine the likely effect of automation upon employment, and therefore on voting, in his area. Yet, fortunately, politics are not only the concern of politicians but necessarily involve   10
the general mass of citizens. It is an urgent political task to educate the people as a whole so as to make them aware of the broad problems and the opportunities of automation.

With the support of public opinion we must strive for a national policy on this issue. One of the bases on which such a policy ought to   15
rest is an organization, perhaps set up jointly by government, industry and trade unions, which would unite sociologists, engineers, economists, experts on labour relations and psychologists, and would engage in a vigorous drive to make people understand the full implications of automation. It should aim at presenting a fair   20

picture, so that the whole problem can be viewed in perspective, from the point of view of the individual, the community and the nation. The man in the street must be given the opportunity to know what is happening, and why, and what part he should play in it.

25 This type of organization would remind industrial workers, for instance, that the mechanized handling of materials has greatly reduced accidents and that ill-health can arise from contact with toxic substances; in other words, that there are many processes more safely done by machines. But it would show that it was well
30 aware of the human problems involved in replacing physical effort by increased responsibility. The fact that not all workers can accept the kind of responsibility which automation would place upon them should not be passed over. The organization would urge the necessity of careful selection of workers, in order to prevent nervous fatigue
35 and possible breakdown. It would provide objective and well-informed long-term forecasts of the types of skill which were likely to be in increasing demand and those which were likely to wither away.

To accelerate the whole pace of modernization with the least
40 possible disturbance to existing institutions and interests, it is essential to have a Minister responsible for this specific task. The Minister should not, as in Russia, be a Minister of Automation, because much more than automation is involved. Perhaps he should be a Minister of Modernization, highly placed in the Cabinet, with
45 power to co-ordinate the policies of other departments in order to reach the main objective.

Answer the following questions which are based on the above passage.

(1) Explain what each of the following words means in its context in the passage. Use either a single word or as short a phrase as possible for each explanation.
concern (line 10)   unite (line 17)   toxic (line 28)
forecasts (line 36)   specific (line 41).

(2) State in your own words the usual attitude towards automation of 'the average Member of Parliament' (lines 5–6).

(3) What is the significance, in the whole argument of the passage, of the sentence, 'The man in the street must be given the opportunity to know what is happening, and why, and what part he should play in it' (lines 23–24)?

Local Government Examinations Board

19. Summarize the following passage in about 250 words.

For several years past, the growth of the supermarket movement has fascinated believers in the need for low-cost distribution, and horrified the advocates of the small shop-keeper. The formula seemed so pre-eminently in tune with the times. It offered so many advantages: large enough units to support scientific management, computerized stock control, and modern merchandising techniques: the economics of bulk buying, mechanical handling and labour-saving operations, passed on to the customer in reduced prices: freedom for the shopper to make her choice undisturbed by the well-meaning attentions of shop assistants: the time-saving advantages of one-stop shopping.

The multiple and co-operative chains which pioneered the new developments could combine, it seemed, the performance of a public service with a highly profitable bonanza for themselves. The manufacturers who supplied them were perhaps not quite so happy. The economies of bulk buying tended sometimes to be at their expense: and there was the everpresent threat that as the supermarket chains grew stronger, they would introduce more of their own private-label brands to compete with the manufacturers' nationally advertised lines.

Nevertheless, here were outlets large and progressive enough to respond, often with dramatic success, to the manufacturer's schemes for in-store merchandising and point of sale promotions. As the supermarkets grew in number, by 300 or so a year, many large manufacturers adapted the structure of their sales forces. They included senior men capable of negotiating special deals and promotions with the supermarket buyers, supported by merchandising teams to work with the store managers on implementing the schemes. Advertising agencies also strengthened their marketing departments with specialists in devising merchandising schemes for supermarkets and self-service stores; at least one agency has sought to extend its experience in this field by acquiring and operating its own small chain of supermarkets.

But this year it has become obvious that the honeymoon is over. Certainly the supermarkets have established themselves as a major factor in grocery retailing. The 1,800 stores now in business, though only about $1\frac{1}{2}$ per cent of all grocery outlets, account between them for something like 15 per cent of grocery turnover; and there is little evidence of the customer resistance to a depersonalized system of shopping that was predicted in the early days. Indeed when some

13,500 smaller self-service stores are added to the 1,800 supermarkets, it is estimated that about 40 per cent of grocery sales are now handled by self-service methods. But the rate of growth has slowed up dramatically.

The main difficulty for the supermarket chains is that High Street rents have become an increasingly formidable item, while the actual saving in manpower from self-service operation has been a good deal less than early theories projected. The expedient of cheap out-of-town sites with vast car parks, on which the economics of the American supermarket are based, is clearly not available in this country. So the pressure to increase store traffic and the average expenditure per customer has intensified—and while one well-sited supermarket can achieve this, three in line sharing the same stretch of High Street pavement and competing with much the same product range and cut-price appeal can find the going very hard.

Moreover the competent middle management, on which the success of a retail chain so largely depends, is just as scarce in this field as in other types of business. Meanwhile the strongest of the independent grocers, once regarded as a dying breed, have made themselves much more formidable competitors, by banding together in voluntary groups and chains, to gain the advantage of greater buying power, joint promotions, and shared management techniques. Manufacturers have learned to treat them just as seriously as the supermarkets, accounting as they do for a rather larger share of grocery turnover than the latter and showing much the same rate of growth.

The pattern of grocery retailing will certainly continue to change over the next ten years, if not as spectacularly as it has during the last ten. But the grand simplicity of a nationwide network of supermarkets, filled in with a few 'mom-and-pop' stores in the back streets and villages, will certainly not be achieved. The manufacturer seeking national distribution will have to think in terms of a mixed economy of shops, and shape his sales force accordingly.

(733 words.)   *The Guardian.*

(1) Using a single word or short phrase, give the meaning of the following words as they are used in the passage:
advocates (line 3)   pre-eminently (line 4)   bonanza (line 14)   projected (line 48)   expedient (line 48).

(2) Explain the meaning of the following phrases as they are used in the passage:
(a) 'one-stop shopping' (line 11)

(b) 'point of sale promotions' (line 23)
  (c) 'depersonalized system of shopping' (lines 39–40).
(3) Explain in your own words the meaning of the following sentences:
  (a) 'But this year it has become obvious that the honeymoon is over' (line 34).
  (b) 'But the grand simplicity of a nationwide network of supermarkets, filled in with a few "mom-and-pop" stores in the back streets and villages, will certainly not be achieved' (lines 69–71).
(4) What threats faced manufacturers with the growth of the supermarket movement?
(5) How did many large manufacturers respond to this increase in the number of supermarkets?
(6) What action did the advertisers take with regard to supermarkets?
(7) State briefly the factors which have contributed to the slowing up of the expansion of supermarkets.
(8) How have the independent grocers combated the supermarkets?

20. (1) Give a clear summary in about 75 words of these letters. This summary should be in the form of a narrative. Supply a heading in which the names and addresses are to be included. (The words in the heading are in addition to the 75 required for the summary).

Hillside,
Cremorne Road,
Seltham,
Hants.
26th August, 19—.

The Manager,
All Britain Touring Coaches,
Winchester.

Dear Sir,
 On the 15th August I travelled by one of your coaches from Ilfracombe to Bristol, where I changed into a second coach leaving for Winchester at 2.15. I left this coach at Seltham and my suitcase was then found to be missing.

At Bristol I understood from the driver that he would see to all the luggage being transferred from one coach to the other, but he evidently did not do so.

Will you please let me know if my suitcase has been sent on to your coach station? It is of brown leatherette, with leather corners and two locks and marked with the initials R.D.F.

Yours faithfully,
R. Finch (Mrs.)

All Britain Touring Coaches,
Winchester.
28th August, 19—

Mrs. R. Finch
Hillside,
Cremorne Road,
Seltham.

Dear Madam,

Thank you for your letter of 26th August.

I am pleased to be able to tell you that your suitcase has been forwarded from the coach station at Bristol to our Lost Property Office here. If it is inconvenient for you to collect it from this office, I will arrange to have it sent to you at Seltham. The coaches for Bristol stop at Seltham Market Cross at 10.30 and 2.30 each day and the suitcase could be put off at whichever time you prefer.

I must, however, point out that, although the drivers of our coaches do in fact stow passengers' cases in the luggage compartment, it is the responsibility of the owners to see that this is done. Your case carried no label of any kind and the driver of the coach has reported to us that he was unable to discover its owner before the departure schedule obliged him to leave Bristol.

Yours faithfully,
S. Abbey.

Hillside,
Cremorne Road,
Seltham,
29th August, 19—.

The Manager,
All Britain Touring Coaches,
Winchester.

Dear Sir,
    I am much obliged to you for your letter of 28th August. I regret having put you to so much trouble about my suitcase, but I had not before travelled by coach and was somewhat bewildered by the noise and bustle of the coach station.

Will you send my case by the morning coach tomorrow, 30th August, and I will be at the Market Cross at 10.30 to receive it?

I should like to express my appreciation of your helpful suggestion to save me the trouble of collecting it myself.

                      Yours faithfully,
                      R. Finch.

Royal Society of Arts.

(2) As secretary to the Managing Director of John Thomas Co., Ltd., Builders' Merchants, prepare a summary of not more than 100 words of the following correspondence. Names and addresses will not be included in the count of words.

                      5 Valley Drive,
                      Bewdley,
                      Worcestershire.
                      29th November, 19–

John Thomas Co., Ltd.,
Meadow Drive,
Kidderminster.

Dear Sirs,
    About six weeks ago I purchased from your firm 12 sheets (8' by 4' by $\frac{1}{4}$") asbestos for the purpose of erecting a garage on the side path of my house at 5 Valley Drive.

I got into touch with an excellent firm of builders, who erected the garage, as far as I could judge, in a most satisfactory manner.

Now I find with the first really wet spell that the rain is causing interior dampness, and some expensive tools which are normally kept on the shelves have been spoiled by rust.

I shall be glad if you will instruct a representative to call at the earliest opportunity in order that he may inspect the garage and arrange for something to be done to remedy the fault.

Yours faithfully,
Simon Betts.

JOHN THOMAS CO., LTD.
Meadow Drive,
Kidderminster.
1st December, 19—.

Simon Betts, Esq.,
5 Valley Drive,
Bewdley, Worcs.

Dear Sir,
    We are very sorry to read in your letter of 29th November that the damp has penetrated your garage and although we are unable to send a representative at the moment, we propose asking our carman to collect one, or part of one, of the sheets so that it can be sent direct to the Technical Department of the manufacturers for inspection. In the meantime we suggest you use a coat of any proprietary brand of water-proofing solution. We recommend Billows & Co., Grade I exterior waterproof liquid.

Yours faithfully,
John Thomas Co., Ltd.

5 Valley Drive,
Bewdley,
Worcestershire.
4th December, 19—.

John Thomas Co., Ltd.,
Meadow Drive,
Kidderminster,

Dear Sir,
    Thank you for your letter of the 1st December. I shall be pleased to let your carman have a small part of one of the asbestos sheets purchased from you and I shall await the manufacturer's report with interest.

Perhaps the carman would bring with him two gallons of Billows & Co.'s Grade I exterior waterproof liquid, which I will pay for on delivery. I shall expect to be reimbursed, of course, if the manufacturers admit liability.

Yours faithfully,
Simon Betts.
Royal Society of Arts.

(3) Give a clear summary in about 100 words of these letters. Supply a heading, in which names and addresses may be included.

F. WHATMOUGH & SONS

227 Oxford Street,
London, W.1.
5th May, 19—.

Messrs. Peabody & Wilkins, Ltd.,
55 West End,
Croydon, Surrey.

Dear Sirs,

On a recent occasion we had the pleasure of a call from your representative, Mr. Adams, who showed us a range of attractive ribbons in nylon, including a new line with a cut edge, which he said was intended to sell at a particularly low figure. This ribbon was not yet, as we understood, in the stage of practical production, but Mr. Adams expected to be able to let us have supplies in red, white, and green in time for the summer trade. Not having heard anything further since his visit, we now write to ask whether we are to be given the opportunity of placing an order within a week or two, and if so at what price.

Yours faithfully,
F. Whatmough & Sons.

PEABODY & WILKINS, LTD.

55 West End,
Croydon, Surrey
7th May, 19—.

Messrs. F. Whatmough & Sons,
227 Oxford Street,
London, W.1.

Dear Sirs,

We are very sorry indeed that you have been kept waiting for details of the nylon cut-edge ribbon shown to you by Mr. Adams last month. Owing to manufacturing difficulties we were until the past few days uncertain as to our ability to offer an acceptable delivery date, but we are now glad to be able to say that the ribbon is ready in the colours you require, and can be supplied in quantities of 10 pieces and over, to retail at 4p. per yard in the $\frac{3}{4}''$ width shown to you, and at 5p. per yard in the $1''$ width. You may look forward to immediate delivery by our own vans upon receipt of your order; our usual terms apply.

Yours faithfully,
Peabody & Wilkins, Ltd.

F. WHATMOUGH & SONS

227 Oxford Street,
London, W.1.
9th May, 19—.

Messrs. Peabody & Wilkins, Ltd.,
55 West End,
Croydon, Surrey.

Dear Sirs,

We are glad to learn from your letter of 7th May that the ribbon for which we enquired is now available. We enclose our order No. P. 1784 for 20 pieces each of the $\frac{3}{4}''$ width in white, red, and green on the distinct understanding that it will be delivered within two days of the date of this letter, on your usual terms.

Yours faithfully,
F. Whatmough & Sons.

Royal Society of Arts.

(4) Give a clear summary in about 100 words of these letters. Supply a heading, in which names and addresses may be included.

18 Millman Lane,
Broadway,
Worcestershire.
7th March, 19—.

W. H. Bourner & Sons, Ltd.,
Builders and Decorators,
Broadway,
Worcestershire.

Dear Sirs,

For some time now I have been having trouble with dampness in one of the bedrooms of my house. This is one of the two rooms which were built on to the older part of the house by your firm some thirty years ago.

When war damage repairs were carried out about five years since, the walls and ceilings were papered. This paper is now peeling off the ceiling and the upper part of one wall, and I can only suppose that this must be due to some rain-water coming through the roof, which is slated over that part of the house. I should be glad if you would send someone to look at the roof and the ceiling, and let me know what measures you would suggest to put the matter right.

Yours faithfully,
H. Wilcox.

W. H. Bourner & Sons, Ltd.,
Builders and Decorators,
Broadway,
Worcestershire.
12th March, 19—.

H. Wilcox, Esq.,
18 Millman Lane,
Broadway,
Worcestershire.

Dear Sir,
    Thank you for your letter of 7th March.
    I was a good deal surprised to hear of the trouble you complained of and I made a personal call on the day I received the letter to see what I could recommend. As you were not at home, your housekeeper allowed me to see the room in question.
    I am glad to say that the cause of the dampness does not seem to be as serious as you supposed. It appears that the room has been occupied with the window and door closed and an electric heater switched on, and, as there is no fireplace, condensation has resulted, which has loosened the paper in the manner you mention. This is difficulty which can be overcome easily by introducing ventilation either by keeping the door and window open to some extent, or by the insertion of a ventilating brick in the wall. Since redecoration will in any case be necessary, the latter method would not cause very great inconvenience, and, since it would provide a permanent remedy, it seems to me to be the best thing to suggest. If you feel able to agree to this, which with the redecoration would cost about £40, perhaps you will let me know as soon as possible, so that the work can be put in hand during the summer months.

Yours faithfully,
W. H. Bourner.

18 Millman Lane,
Broadway,
Worcestershire.
14th March, 19—.

W. H. Bourner & Sons, Ltd.,
Builders and Decorators,
Broadway,
Worcestershire.

Dear Sirs,

    I am very glad to have your letter of 12th March, and I have read your remarks with interest.

If you are really confident that your suggestion would, if carried out, dispose of the dampness once and for all, I shall be glad if you will put the work in hand as soon as possible.

Please let me have at least three days' notice of the date you propose to begin.

Yours faithfully,
H. Wilcox.
Royal Society of Arts.

7. Writing business letters

The importance of the business letter

Although many commercial transactions are conducted by means of the telephone, the letter is still the most important form of communication between one firm and another. It provides a permanent record of business arrangements and avoids the necessity for personal contact between the correspondents.

Goodwill between business concerns is stimulated and fostered more often through correspondence than through personal contact. Some businessmen devote much of their time solely to the writing of letters. This provides an indication of the value which must be attached to business correspondence.

Presentation of the business letter

The letter-head

Even the smallest firm has its own headed note-paper. The name of the firm is usually printed across the top of the note-paper; the address may come either directly below the name or on the right-hand side. The telephone number and telegraphic address may appear on the left hand side, opposite the address.

Date

The date should be typed on the right-hand side, allowing a small space to separate it from the address, if that is also on the right-hand side. The date should be given with the day of the month, the month, and the year. The month ought never to be abbreviated.

4th September, 1966.

Note that a comma is necessary to separate the month from the year, but the full stop after the year can be omitted. There is a growing tendency in some firms to arrange the date as 4 September, 1966, but for the time being, students should adopt the more usual form.

Reference

Very often the printed heading includes a reference line; otherwise any reference number is placed on the left-hand side opposite the date. This is usually in the form of a code either relating to the departmental filing system, or giving an indication of the writer of the letter. Thus F.T.C./S.J.B. would suggest that F.T.C. are the initials of the writer and S.J.B. are the initials of the typist.

A reply to a letter should always quote the reference number as this aids the rapid delivery of letters within a business to the person for whom they are intended.

Inside address

The name and address of the recipient must appear either on the left-hand side on a level immediately below the date, or at the foot of the letter. Sometimes their position is designed to coincide with a cellophane window in an envelope, so that they act as the outside address as well. Otherwise, except for local Government and certain Civil Service letters, the name and address of the addressee will usually precede the salutation at the top of the letter.

This address is used for record purposes and enables the secretary to place letters in the correct envelopes.

Note. (a) 'Messrs.' is used only when personal names appear in the title of the firm; often it is omitted even in this instance. It must never be applied to a limited company.

(b) 'Esq.' (the abbreviated form of 'Esquire') has now lost most of its courteous significance, although it still retains a certain complimentary tone. It can be used only when the initials of the addressee are known. Otherwise 'Mr.' must be applied. 'Esq.' and 'Mr.' must never appear together.

(c) The words 'street', 'road', 'square', 'crescent', etc., should not be abbreviated, but the customary abbreviations for the names of counties may be used.

(d) It is customary now to type the name of the town in capital letters.

(e) Whenever possible, letters to firms should be addressed to the senior official of the department for which they are intended. This will save unnecessary delay.

Salutation

'Dear Sir' or 'Dear Sirs' is the usual form for business letters. Whether married or unmarried, women should be addressed as 'Dear Madam'. If the correspondents are personally acquainted or there is a reason for the writer's wishing to appear informal, 'Dear Mr., Mrs., or Miss ——' will be used as appropriate.

'Sir' and 'Sirs' are reserved for very formal letters.

Subject heading

A subject heading is sometimes inserted at the top of the letter itself after the salutation. This enables the recipient to classify the correspondence and relate it to previous letters concerning the same matter. A subject heading should be used only when it will serve such a purpose. Account number of hire-purchase firms, building societies, and other organizations are better included in a heading, and manufacturers often quote the order number as a heading in their correspondence.

Complimentary close

The customary business letter which begins with 'Dear Sir', should close with 'Yours faithfully'. For the personal letter which opens with 'Dear Mr. ——', 'Yours sincerely' is the usual complimentary close. 'Yours truly' is a useful alternative to 'Yours sincerely' when the writer wishes to be informal but has no personal acquaintance with his correspondent. It can come at the end of a letter which has begun with either 'Dear Sir' or 'Dear Mr. ——'.

With two writers who are close friends 'With kind regards' is sometimes inserted before 'Yours sincerely'. 'Yours very truly' 'Yours very sincerely' are occasionally used but seem unnecessarily effusive.

If the final sentence of the letter begins with a present participle, it is often continued into the complimentary close.

> 'Trusting that your venture will prove successful,
> we remain,
>   Yours faithfully,'

N.B. A comma, not a full stop, is necessary after 'successful'; a full-stop would produce an unrelated participle 'trusting'.

'Sincerely yours' is frequently used in America but should be avoided in this country. 'Your obedient servant' was at one time a standard phrase used by Civil Service departments but it is almost obsolete today.

Signature

The manner of signing letters differs from one organization to another.

(a) Sometimes the person responsible signs his name, indicating his designation or position.

> *Yours faithfully,*
> *T. Tallis*
> *(Secretary)*

(b) The name of the firm may be added after the complimentary close.

> *Yours faithfully,*
> THOMAS ATTWOOD AND COMPANY LIMITED,
> *J. Baldwin,*
> *Secretary.*

(c) When someone signs the letter on behalf of the firm or higher official, the abbreviation p.p. (Latin: *per procurationem*) is added.

> *p.p. Thomas Attwood and Co., Ltd.*

This custom is being replaced by the word 'for'

> *for Thomas Attwood and Co., Ltd.*

(d) Certain organizations, especially banks and insurance companies, consider it unnecessary to add their name after the complimentary close if the letter is on headed note-paper.

Enclosures

As an indication to the sender and the recipient that the letter is accompanied by enclosures, the abbreviation 'Enc.' is typed at the bottom left-hand corner of the letter.

A postscript should not be added to a business letter. The letter must be rewritten to include the extra material.

Specimen business letter

JOHN TAVERNER AND COMPANY, LTD.

Telephone: 01.667.1531   14 Bridge Street,
Telegrams: Taverner London.   London, E.C.4.
Ref. GTF/FS   6th April, 19—.

Orlando Gibbons and Son,
74 Stafford Road,
Leeds 8.

Dear Sirs,

<u>Fire Damage at 74 Stafford Road</u>

As a result of our representative's interview with you on 27th April, 19—, we suggest settlement of your claim at £246.

If you agree to this figure, please sign and return the enclosed Acceptance Form to us.

                 Yours faithfully,
             JOHN TAVERNER AND CO.
                   G. Farnaby.
                     Manager.

Enc.

The content of the letter

The effective business letter should influence the reader and induce action. Therefore, the writer must be not only technically equipped for the task, but also acutely aware of the effect his words will have upon the recipient.

The three important factors which must be considered in business correspondence are:

     (a) clarity,
     (b) courtesy,
     (c) conciseness.

Remember that for all businessmen, time is precious. Keep your letters brief but polite, and avoid complicated words when simple words will suffice. It is wise to write short paragraphs in letters as they will be easily and quickly understood. This will save time especially if the letter is referred to after the initial reading.

Before you begin to write any letter, you must determine its precise purpose. You should marshal your material so that the object of the letter will be immediately clear to the reader. Consider the reader of your letter in everything you say. If you are replying to a letter, make certain you answer all the queries raised. Remember throughout that your letter *is* a reply, and adopt a helpful attitude in satisfying the requests.

The opening paragraph

Keep the first paragraph brief. If the letter is a reply to one you have received, thank the writer and refer to the date when the letter was written, *not* when you received it. It is also preferable to mention briefly the subject matter.

Dear Sir,
>*Thank you for your letter of 6th May regarding your proposed holiday in Greece.*

This simple and direct approach avoids the unsuitable clichés which are now considered out of date, such as

'I beg to inform you that . . .'

The body of the letter

Organize the material for your letter so that it follows a logical sequence. If your letter is a reply to one you have received, begin by answering the points raised. Make certain you have satisfied all the requests before introducing new ideas.

In some business letters the paragraphs are numbered. This is used especially when technical details such as estimates and specifications are included. It is, however, better to avoid this method except where it will provide greater clarity for the reader.

The closing paragraph

Many letters require a closing courtesy sentence. This will balance the opening sentence and should be set out as a separate paragraph.

If you require any further details, I shall be pleased to provide them for you.

Make certain that this final sentence is complete, and does not contain merely a present participle phrase. 'Trusting we shall hear from you soon.' is a phrase not a sentence.

It is tactful in a letter of apology to repeat your regrets at the end of the letter, but in wording which is different from the first apology.

Except for letters dealing with technical matters, the last paragraph should not be a summary of the rest of the letter.

Types of business letter

In general, business letters fall into one of the following categories:

Letter requesting information

Before writing to ask for information check that your request is reasonable. If so, make sure that your specific requirements are clear, so that no misunderstanding can arise. You must write courteously since you are taking up the time of someone who may have no obligation to assist you.

It will also help the recipient of your letter if you explain why you require the information. In this way, he may be able to serve you more satisfactorily.

Dear Sir,

I should be glad if you would send me your catalogue of music for sale.

I am particularly interested in buying the orchestral parts of modern works for large symphony orchestra.

Yours faithfully,

Letter providing information

If possible avoid the necessity for lengthy correspondence. Make certain that the information is complete and satisfies all the requirements of the original letter.

Dear Sir,

We are enclosing our latest catalogue of orchestral parts for sale which you requested in your letter of 6th June. The items marked with an asterisk are at present out of stock. We can supply them to order in about three weeks.

Postage is chargeable at the rate of 10p in the £ on all orders.

Yours faithfully,

Enc.

Letter of complaint

The purpose of a letter of complaint is to obtain an apology or redress for the fault committed. You must concentrate exclusively upon the matter under consideration. Any digression into irrelevancies at once weakens your case.

The emotional element of your writing must be tempered with reason; if your letter betrays vindictiveness or uncontrolled fury, your complaint will receive less sympathetic treatment. Allegations must be supported by evidence.

At the end of the letter, you must make clear to your reader what action you expect him to take.

Dear Sir,

    Under separate cover, I am returning a blanket which I bought at your store on Saturday 17th September. When I unpacked it at home, I discovered that there was a large tear in it.

As I intend this blanket as a wedding present, I should be glad if you would replace it at once, or refund me the full cost.

Yours faithfully,

Letter of apology

Whether the complaint against you is justified or not, reply as soon as possible. If investigations have to be made into the causes of the complaint, do not use this as an excuse for delaying your reply.

If the complaint is unjustified, give your explanation without a sense of self-righteousness or injured pride. If the person complaining has suffered an inconvenience or loss, express regret even though you are in no way to blame.

If the complaint *is* justifiable, make your apology sincerely and clearly, offering whatever remedy is possible, or enquiring into the cause of the trouble. Avoid an air of reluctance in accepting the complaint if you have no genuine defence. Give assurances of greater care in the future.

Remember that for many business organizations, especially those concerned with retail distribution, it is more satisfactory regarding customer relations, and ultimately less trouble and cost, to accept a complaint and offer compensation, than to dispute the case.

Dear Madam,

    We very much regret that the blanket you bought from us was defective. As these blankets are wrapped in polythene covers by the manufacturer, we were unable to notice this fault. However, we have notified the manufacturer and have made arrangements to send you a replacement at once.

We are enclosing a postal order to cover the cost of postage on the returned blanket. Once again we apologize for the inconvenience you have been caused, and we hope that the replacement will prove entirely satisfactory.

Yours faithfully,

Circular letter

A circular differs in several respects from the customary business letter. It carries the heading of the organization and its address but usually does not include the name and address of the recipient since it is often not practicable to address thousands of copies of a circular individually.

Although the circular may be distributed to thousands of people, you must not forget that it is read by individual people, so that you must still adopt a personal style. Advertisers are increasingly making use of the printed circular where there is often a deliberate attempt to make it appear as though it were written by hand.

At the end of a circular, the writer should make it clear what position he holds in the organization which gives him power to write on their behalf—Chairman, Secretary, Treasurer, etc.

ST. PAUL'S LODGE

6th October, 19—

Dear Sir,
    I am writing to you in the hope that you will help us to raise £5,000 for the rebuilding of our rest home for old people.

The structure of St. Paul's Lodge is now over one hundred years old and immediate repairs are necessary.

I write to you on behalf of the twenty elderly folk here who will have to leave if we cannot collect the required sum of money.

Please give as generously as you can.

Yours faithfully,
J. Sinclair.
(*Secretary*).

Letter to a newspaper

Letters to a newspaper must be addressed to the Editor. Although you may hope your letter will be printed in the correspondence column for the benefit of the readers, you must write it to the Editor himself. He acts in the same capacity as a chairman in a debate. Your remarks are addressed to him, although what you say is naturally intended for others to read.

Letter of Application

Although many firms require candidates to complete an application form for jobs offered, a letter of application is still often necessary. The way such a letter is composed may itself make the difference between acceptance or rejection.

The opening paragraph should refer to the post for which you are applying and where you saw the advertisement.

Details of date of birth, education, qualifications and experience might be better given on a separate sheet of paper. You should also provide the names and addresses of two people who are prepared to act as referees on your behalf. Always ask permission of these people before you use their names in this respect.

Dear Sir,

In reply to your advertisement in the Evening Herald, I wish to apply for the post of clerical assistant.

I give details of my education, qualifications and experience on the attached sheet. I have also included the names of two people who have agreed to act as referees.

If there is any further information you require, I shall be pleased to provide it.

Yours sincerely,

Name:	*Andrew Williams*
Address:	*16 Linden Lea,* *Wenlock Edge,* *Staffs.*
Education:	*Clun High School 1965–72* *Teme Valley Technical College 1972–73*
Qualifications:	*G.C.E. 'O' level:* *English* *History* *French* *Mathematics* *General Science*
	R.S.A.: *Principles of Accounts Stage II*
Referees:	*Mr. Charles Ives, B.Com.,* *Head of Business Studies Department,* *Teme Valley Technical College*
	Mr. Carl Ruggles, *16 Carter Avenue,* *Hadley, Staffs.*

Memorandum

A memorandum is a letter, usually dealing with one specific topic, which is sent internally within an organization.

At the head of the memorandum the writer must indicate from whom it comes and for whom it is intended, with a brief heading of the subject matter and the date.

The salutation and complimentary close are omitted, but in other respects the memorandum is composed like a letter. It is usually written on special 'memo' paper (8" × 5") which may be headed.

MEMORANDUM

To: Mr. Jenkins Date: 16th May, 19—
From: Mr. South

Travelling Expenses

Head Office has issued new regulations regarding travelling expenses. I should be glad if you would come to my office on Friday morning to discuss this matter.

B.S.

EXERCISES

1. A local youth club is organizing a dance and has written to ask for the use of a hall for which you are responsible. The dance is to be in aid of a very worthy charity, but the youth club has a reputation for rowdiness and lack of discipline. Write a suitable reply to the request in about 150 words.

L.G.E.B.

2. As secretary to a firm which has recently had one of its factories damaged by fire, write a letter to the Chairman of the Board of Directors, who is abroad, giving him a full account of the damage and its immediate effect upon production.

Corporation of Secretaries (Intermediate).

3. As secretary to a departmental store write a letter to a customer who has fallen behind with his payments on a hire purchase account. The customer has always paid promptly on previous hire purchase accounts.

4. From 10th to 17th February you will be attending a conference in Lowestoft on 'Mechanization in the Fishing Industry'. Write to the Esplanade Hotel booking a room with bath at a moderate cost.

5. You were promised delivery of a new typewriter within ten days of placing the order. It is now three weeks since the order was placed, but the new machine has not been delivered. Write a letter of complaint to the suppliers.
London Chamber of Commerce (Private Secretary's Diploma).

6. Write a letter to your local newspaper objecting to the proposed erection of a block of flats in your district. Give reasons why the plan should be abandoned.

7. Write a letter to your employer or to some appropriate superior in your company applying for promotion and giving reasons in support of your application.
Institute of Transport (Graduate).

8. Write a letter to the headmaster of the school you attended requesting permission to use his name as a referee for a post for which you are applying.

9. Write a letter of application for the post of management trainee with the Westbrook Publishing Company. Give details of your education and experience and any other information which may be of use to the firm in making their selection for an interview.

10. You have been offered and have accepted the post of management trainee with the Westbrook Publishing Company. Write a letter to one of those who provided a reference for you thanking him for his help and giving brief details of the post.

11. Write a letter to your bank manager requesting a bank loan of £450 to pay for the installation of central heating in your home. Give details of intended repayments and length of time the loan is required.

12. Write a reply from the bank manager to the above letter.

13. Write to your insurance company reporting damage caused by a broken water pipe in the roof of your house.

14. As secretary to a car-hire firm, write to the advertising manager of your local newspaper asking for information regarding advertising

costs. Give details of the advertisement you wish to insert in the newspaper.

15. Write a letter to the secretary of a local youth club declining an invitation to speak to the members. Offer to give the talk at a later date.

16. As secretary to a society of your own choice, write to a local dignitary inviting him to be a vice-president.

17. Write a letter to the principal of a technical college giving an estimate for the supply of stationery.

18. Write a letter to a business acquaintance explaining that you are unable to keep an appointment with him. Suggest an alternative date and time.

19. Write a letter in reply to a customer who has complained that a dining-room table she bought from your shop was badly scratched when it was delivered.

20. Write a letter inviting prospective customers to a special showing of the new French motor car the 'Rapide' for which you are sole agents in the area.

21. As a travel agent, write a circular letter to be sent to local schools offering your services as organizers of school party visits abroad. Give brief details of sample holidays with costs, etc.

22. The Good Works Association of which you are secretary has decided to build a new social centre for the use of old people. Write a letter for circulation among the general public appealing for funds.
Corporation of Secretaries (Intermediate).

23. As secretary to your Village Association, write a circular letter to be sent to all new residents giving details of the amenities offered and encouraging them to join the Association.

24. Your firm intends to move out of London to a small town in the Home Counties. Write a circular letter to be sent to all employees giving details of the plan, a description of the town and its amenities, and requesting the views of the staff.

25. Your local council has decided to increase the proportion of the rates to be spent on the library. Use of the library services is free to all local residents who obtain a ratepayer's signature. Write a letter of about 150 words to be sent to all ratepayers, explaining the increase and encouraging wider use of these services.

L.G.E.B.

26. Write a letter to your local authority applying for the tenancy of a council house.

27. A sudden increase in your quarterly gas bill causes you to suspect that a mistake has been made. Write a letter to the Gas Board.

28. Write a memorandum to a junior clerk asking him to bring certain correspondence files to your office on the following morning.

29. Write a memorandum to a junior clerk asking him to prepare records of the cost of postage on letters sent by the department during the past six weeks.

30. Write a memorandum to Mr. Howes asking him to prepare a timetable for the forthcoming Conference on Business Machines. Give brief instructions how this timetable should be laid out.

31. Write a memorandum to all heads of departments calling a meeting on Tuesday at 10.30 a.m.

32. As production manager in a music publishers, write a memorandum to the Retail Department drawing attention to an increase in the price of certain items in the catalogue.

8. Business reports and meetings

Routine reports

A report is a document containing a detailed examination of a situation or problem, setting out the relevant information, findings, and conclusions. Often, but not always, recommendations are made in the light of the conclusions for action to be taken. The purpose of most reports is to enable the executive authority to take decisions regarding the matters under review.

There are basically two types of business report. The first is the formal routine report such as one prepared by the secretary of a company for the Annual General Meeting of shareholders.

This kind of report opens with a formal statement of the time and place of the meeting.

The 64th Annual General Meeting of Stevenson Engineering Company Limited was held on 5th October, 19—, at the Orion Hotel, Eastleigh, Mr. John Greene (Chairman) presiding.

The report itself gives an account of the firm's activities during the past year with particular emphasis on any new developments since the previous Annual General Meeting. If possible the secretary will refer to future prospects, but will not put forward any personal opinions unless his comments reflect the agreed policy of the directors.

The report itself will conclude with the adoption of the accounts and approval of the declared dividend. Any changes amongst the directors will also be mentioned.

Meeting report

In the report of a meeting, the heading will also contain details of the place where it was held and the names of those who attended, specifying who was Chairman. Such a report will be written in the third person and in the past tense.

Poolmouth Public Library
Report of discussion regarding the increased allocation of funds.

A meeting of the Library Committee was held in the Chief Librarian's office on 14th January 19—.

Present
Mr. R. V. Williams: Chief Librarian
                      (*in the chair*)
Mrs. E. Smyth: Librarian
Mr. R. Quilter: Assistant Librarian
Mr. W. Hurlstone: Assistant Librarian

Mr. Williams reported that an additional £500 had been granted to the library for the purchase of books for the reference library.

The second type of report is one requested on a particular subject.

Special reports

All reports require a heading giving the date and brief details of the subject. The names of those to whom the report is to be sent may appear either at the top of the first page or at the bottom of the last.

Individual reports or memoranda

Depending upon the subject, an individual report may be written in narrative form with the possible use of the first person.

To: Mr. P. Humphrey   14th January, 19—
Ref: AB/LC 564

Revision of Mailing List
In response to your request of 6th January to revise our mailing list, I retained only the names of those customers who have placed orders with us during the past twelve months.

Business reports

The directors or senior management in a firm may ask for an enquiry into a certain matter. It will be the duty of the secretary or another responsible person to write a report when the enquiry is completed. Sometimes the enquiry will be referred to a committee. In this case, the secretary will be required to attend the meetings of the committee and draft the report from notes he has taken at the meetings.

The person preparing the report must establish in his own mind the purpose and scope of the report. He needs to determine precisely what information is required by those who will read his work.

He will examine the situation in question, gathering relevant material evidence and taking notice of opinions and comments which may be of importance in arriving at conclusions.

When the investigation is finished, it will be his duty to collate the evidence and prepare the report so that it is easily and quickly understood by those who asked for it to be made.

The purpose of a report is to present the required information so that those who have requested it can take action upon the recommendations which the report contains. Therefore the writer must make a balanced judgement from the various opinions he has examined.

Presentation of the report

Each item of the report should be set out as a separate paragraph, which should be numbered for ease of reference.

Introduction

The author may insert a short introduction explaining why the report has been written and making brief reference to the problems examined.

Terms of reference

The report itself begins with a clear statement of the purpose and scope of the enquiry. The terms of reference are the instructions you have been given determining the exact subject of the report. The success of a report depends upon the writer's knowing the exact object of the study. The name(s) of the person(s) commissioning the report may also appear in the terms of reference.

Evidence

The information obtained must be carefully sorted and arranged in a logical order. This may be presented either chronologically or in sequence determined by the subject matter. Specific details need to be quoted, but statistical evidence and tabulated data are better included in an appendix at the end of the report; their inclusion in the body of the text can create unnecessary complications for the reader.

It is in this section that the writer must exercise discrimination. Only information which has a direct bearing on the recommendations to be made later ought to be mentioned.

Findings

As a result of the evidence he has gathered, the writer will derive certain conclusions. In this section the differing opinions on the subject need to be clarified and if possible reconciled. Estimates of results and costs of proposed plans need to be given.

Recommendations

In the light of the facts and findings, the writer will make his recommendations. He will suggest which course of action should be taken, and will indicate the results likely to occur if his advice is taken.

If the report is of considerable length, the author may give a summary of his findings and recommendations at the end but usually this is necessary only if the subject is too complicated to be easily retained in the mind of the reader.

Some organizations, however, always require a summary on one page, giving a brief outline of the entire report, including the terms of reference, the factual evidence, the findings and the recommendations. This digest is submitted with the report itself.

Meetings

The secretary of every organization has the responsibility for making the necessary preparations for holding a meeting, whether it is an annual general meeting, a committee meeting, or a board meeting of directors.

He must first arrange a suitable time and place. It is advisable to check before finally fixing the time and place that most of those who are entitled to attend will be able to do so.

Preparing the agenda

When these arrangements have been settled, the secretary prepares the agenda. In consultation with the chairman, he will draw up a list of items to be considered and arrange them in a suitable order. This requires careful consideration so that matters dependent upon each other are grouped together and placed in the correct sequence. The routine business of the meeting will come first.

The agenda of almost every meeting will begin with a reference to the minutes of the previous meeting. If these have been circularized earlier, they will usually be taken as read. Matters arising from these minutes will be dealt with next. The remaining items will be arranged according to the purpose of the meeting. The following is an outline of a characteristic agenda for a board or committee meeting.

1. *Minutes of the meeting held on 17th October, 19—.*
2. *Correspondence.*
3. *Authorization of cheque payment.*
4. *Report of sub-committee.*
5. *Financial business.*
6. *General business.*
7. *Date of next meeting.*
8. *Any other business.**

At an annual general meeting it is customary to follow the minutes with a report from the chairman or secretary. After this comes the treasurer's report which presents a statement of the accounts. The final part of routine business is the election of officers to serve for the coming year. The remaining items on the agenda will cover matters brought forward for discussion.

Such an agenda would appear as follows.

* In Scotland this is termed 'Any other competent business' (A.O.C.B.).

1. *Minutes of the previous Annual General Meeting held on 17th October, 19—.*
2. *Chairman's report.*
3. *Treasurer's report.*
4. *Election of officers.*
5. *Next season's programme of events.*
6. *Any other business.*

Convening the meeting

Once the agenda is agreed by the chairman, the secretary sends a copy of it to each person entitled to attend the meeting. It is the duty of the secretary to see that this is carried out in good time before the meeting. In most cases the rules of the society or organization will specify the length of notice to be given. Otherwise the usual period of time is seven clear days before the meeting.

Any member wishing to make a proposal to be included in the agenda must, therefore, contact the secretary at least ten days before the meeting. This will also apply to nominations for officers to serve on the committee, but each society will have its own rules regarding procedure in the matter. The section 'Any other business' should not cover matters of major importance. Proper notice should be given for such items to be included in the agenda itself.

The notification of the meeting is usually presented in the form of a letter from the secretary. This should state clearly the date, time, and place of the meeting; often the letter will be read aloud by the secretary at the beginning of the meeting.

The chairman

If the regular chairman of the organization or society is not present, a chairman must be appointed before the meeting can commence. The chairman* is the most important person since he should have complete control over the conduct of the meeting. With skill, he is able to promote lively discussions and can focus the divergent views of the speakers on the task of making decisions. He should be certain that he is completely familiar with the matters to be debated. Therefore it is important that he should make advance preparations once the agenda has been settled.

Although the chairman should talk little unless required, the attitude he adopts will influence all those present. A business-like

* In Scotland, the chairman is called the Convener.

approach in handling matters and in the way he directs the proceedings will be of utmost importance.

Before the meeting begins the chairman must be satisfied that a quorum is present, and that the meeting is conducted in accordance with the rules. If necessary, he must decide on points of order raised. As well as maintaining order, he should prevent irrelevant arguments. The chairman will also ask for motions from members and will put them to the vote after discussion. From time to time, it may be necessary for him to sum up the different views put forward in order to bring the attention of the meeting back to the subject when speakers have digressed from it.

Although the chairman presides at the meeting, the secretary still has a number of responsibilities. He must provide any necessary documents and may be consulted by the chairman. Also he must take notes of the meeting so that he can write the minutes afterwards.

Minutes

Minutes are a concise written record of the business transacted at a meeting, the decisions reached, and the action to be taken. Usually the minutes are not a report of the meeting since the actual discussion is not noted, although some organizations prefer to keep a fuller account of the proceedings and will wish to include reference to views expressed by the speakers, including also the names of proposers of motions and other such details.

Each minute should be numbered as a separate item. This makes cross-reference and indexing much simpler.

The minutes should open with a brief record of the time and place of the meeting and those present. Apologies for absence must also be noted. The minutes themselves will appear in chronological order as an account of the transactions of the meeting. At the end, the secretary should note in the minutes the time that the meeting ended.

At the next meeting of the committee, the minutes of the previous meeting may be read aloud by the secretary. To save time and to allow members to study them in detail, the minutes of the previous meeting are often circulated beforehand. In this case they are not read aloud at the meeting. With the approval of those present, the chairman will sign them as a true record of the proceedings of the previous meeting.

After the meeting, it will be the responsibility of the secretary to see that the resolutions passed are put into effect.

The writer of minutes must take adequate notes at the meeting; considerable skill is needed to be able to distinguish at once between relevant and irrelevant resolutions. In the meeting itself, selection of material must be made in order to simplify the task of compiling the minutes from the notes taken.

Distinction must be made between minutes of narration which summarize statements made by members, and minutes of resolution where specific proposals are made. The proposer and seconder of all motions must be named and the outcome of any vote or decision made explicit.

The following is a typical example of an extract from the minutes of a committee meeting.

1. The Minutes of the meeting *held on 14th July 19— were taken as read, approved and signed.*

2. Matters arising from the minutes

It was not possible to book the Granton Ballroom for the dinner-dance on September 1st as proposed. The Secretary had made arrangements with the Star Assembly Rooms who could accommodate up to 100 guests and are able to provide a buffet supper on September 1st. The meeting approved of the alteration of plans.

3. Treasurer

As had been expected, Mr. Milton has resigned as Treasurer since he has left the district to live in Bristol. The Chairman proposed Mr. Henry Lawes to take the post of Treasurer and was seconded by Miss Jenny Lind. The meeting agreed to the appointment of Mr. Lawes.

EXERCISES

1. You have been asked to enquire into the circumstances in which an accident has occurred. Write a report in which you indicate what you consider to be the facts of the case and state what evidence has led you to your conclusions.

Institute of Transport (Graduate).

2. You are secretary to an old and rather conservative firm which has hitherto experienced very little serious competition in its particular type of product. Recently, however, a new firm has entered the same field of business and has succeeded in capturing a considerable portion of your firm's custom. The Board of Directors has asked you to investigate what action can be taken to retrieve some of your firm's lost trade. Write the report.

Corporation of Secretaries (Intermediate).

3. As an insurance assessor, you have inspected a house damaged by water from a burst pipe. Write a report to be submitted to the insurance company.

4. Assume you are hon. secretary of a social club. Write a report for the information of members summarizing your committee's plans for the remainder of the year, giving brief reasons for the inclusion of the items to which you refer.
London Chamber of Commerce (Private Secretary's Certificate).

5. The chairman of the company for which you work is investigating ways in which office procedure could be made more efficient. He is considering in particular, the introduction of new equipment and the reorganization of staff duties. He wishes to know the views of employees on these matters. Write a memorandum to the chairman, of about 200 words, indicating your ideas and giving reasons for any changes you may suggest.
Chartered Institute of Secretaries (Intermediate).

6. You have been sent by the head of your department to inspect the work of a branch office of your undertaking. Write a short report informing him of the results of your inspection.
Institute of Transport (Graduate).

7. Imagine that you are secretary of a company that sells goods direct to consumers, and that your directors are considering whether to increase prices so as to make a bigger profit on each item sold at a risk of diminishing sales or to cut prices and increase total profits by selling more goods. Write a memorandum for the board, setting out the arguments for each policy. Make your memorandum as clear and practical as you can, and for the purpose of the question imagine that your company is selling any article you wish.
Corporation of Secretaries (Intermediate).

8. Your employer wishes to purchase some new equipment for your office. Write a report suggesting three items to replace ones you have at present which are inadequate. Give your reasons for the recommendations.

9. You have spent a week at a hotel recommended in the Hotel Guide. Write a report for the Editor of this publication which will enable him to assess the present standards there for the forthcoming revised edition of the Guide.

10. You have been asked to examine the work of a goods depôt, and during your inspection you have made the following brief notes: 'staff unpunctual'—'goods handled carefully'—'records not properly kept'—'manager conscientious, works hard'—'too much overtime worked'—'working conditions of staff should be improved'—'some discourtesy to enquirers'. Write the report you would submit, basing it on these notes.
Institute of Transport (Graduate).

11. Outline briefly the duties of a secretary in preparing for a meeting.

12. Outline briefly the responsibilities of a chairman at a meeting.

13. What is the purpose of recording minutes of meetings?

14. Prepare an agenda for the Annual General Meeting of a Students Union. Include three items for discussion at the meeting.

15. Write a letter to all the members of a music society giving notice of the Annual General Meeting and urging them to attend.

16. Explain briefly the meaning of the following terms:
    (1) a standing committee
    (2) an *ad hoc* committee
    (3) a sub-committee
    (4) an agenda
    (5) a quorum
    (6) a co-opted committee member
    (7) a point of order
    (8) an amendment
    (9) standing orders
    (10) a proxy vote
    (11) a casting vote
    (12) an extraordinary general meeting.

17. Your firm is proposing to install some modern machinery, which will call for reorganization among the workers. (You may imagine any details you like.) You are acting as a secretary to a joint committee, representing the management and the workers, which is discussing the proposal. Write the minutes of a meeting of this committee.
Corporation of Secretaries (Intermediate).

18. Draft a notice convening the Annual General Meeting of a merchant shipping company. Prepare the agenda for this meeting.

19. From the given notes, write suitable minutes for a committee meeting.

Conference: 16 May agreed. Mount Royal Hotel Ballroom.
    9.30 Introduction. Mr. Copland presiding.
           R. Harris: Management by Objectives.
   10.30 Coffee in lounge
   11.00 Questions and discussion.
           Vote of thanks: L. Foss
   12.15 Lunch
    1.30 W. Schuman: Decision and Control
           Discussion.
    3.00 Tea

Arrangements: S. Barber to provide duplicated material.
Secretary to see
   1. Caretakers: chairs
   2. Caterers: lunch and coffee
   3. Hanson Electronic: Public address.
Treasurer: payment of £25 fee + expenses each to Mr. Harris and Mr. Schuman.

20. From these notes, write suitable minutes for a club committee meeting.

Minutes: read and approved.
V. Thomson suggested subscription rise from £3 to £5 would deter new members.
H. Cowell stated increase needed to maintain programme of events.
Motion to increase. Prop. H. Cowell, Seconded J. K. Paine Passed 6 to 2.
Newsletter approved for distribution.
Advert in Evening Record for new members, Sept. 16.
Secretary to investigate cost and to draft wording.
Dinner–Dance: J. Cage suggested Manor House Hotel.
Secretary to investigate cost for 60, 80, 100 guests.
Menus? Sept. 28 or 29.
Next Meeting: 22nd Aug., Club House, 8.0 p.m.

9. Effective speaking

Getting the most out of discussion

In the sphere of business, many people spend a considerable part of their time attending meetings where matters regarding the administration and policy of the company are discussed. At committee meetings, once the formal part of the agenda has been passed, the remaining time is devoted to the discussion of the other items.

In order to make a personal contribution on such occasions, it is necessary to understand precisely the points under debate. Then you need to analyse your own views in relationship to those of the other people present.

In these circumstances you should bear the following points in mind:

1. Beware of generalizations which can result in much of your argument being based on falsities. Those who disagree with you will find it easy to disprove your generalizations by quoting particular examples which contradict what you say.

2. Always produce evidence to support your statements of

facts and opinion. This will add force to your arguments and will enable others to appreciate your views more easily.

3. Distinguish between emotion and logical argument. Emotion is bound to enter to some degree and influence you strongly in some instances, but you must recognize this as such. Do not confuse emotional reaction to a provocative subject with rational thought.

4. Always try to see the other person's point of view even if you disagree violently with what he believes. Only by understanding why he holds opposing opinions will you have any hope of changing these opinions. This is particularly relevant in business matters. It applies also to subjects of a controversial nature regarding deeply rooted prejudices and convictions—religious beliefs, politics, profound moral issues such as capital punishment and blood sports—subjects on which intelligent people clearly take sides, and are inclined to offer no compromise or to see any worth in opposing opinions.

5. It is justifiable to be neutral regarding a controversial subject, but this neutrality should be positive and exist only after you have considered the views of both sides and see value in certain aspects of each. Only a fanatic will think that the major issues of today, concerning religion, politics, and social conscience, are simple and clearly defined. However, we must avoid the apathy and laziness which affect so many people attending committee meetings and discussion groups who retire into a complacency which implies an immunity from the responsibility to think. This kind of neutrality is entirely negative.

Discussing the topic

When you are about to speak:
(1) consider only the matter in question,
(2) determine the relevance of the points you wish to make,
(3) do not repeat what others have already said except to show support for a proposal,
(4) estimate the value of what you have to say upon the case you support or the decision which has to be made,
(5) keep your remarks brief and do not digress onto another topic which concerns something else.

The value of discussion in business

In all aspects of business, it is vital to be able to see the other person's point of view in order to sell him your ideas. Similarly you must be prepared to accept his opinions even where they conflict with your own, if the situation will benefit as a result. The businessman who has dogmatic preconceived notions and will never yield to the ideas of others is prejudicing his own chances of success since co-operation becomes very difficult. Nevertheless, one should not have such shallow beliefs that they change at the slightest suggestion from another person.

There is almost always an element of truth to be found in the firm convictions of one who holds contrary opinions to our own.

Informal discussion

In the previous chapter, we have seen the importance of the chairman at a meeting (see page 138). An informal discussion can be conducted on the lines of a committee meeting, with each member taking an equal part. The chairman controls the procedure and stimulates discussion of the subject by encouraging those present to air their views.

There need be no actual motion proposed, but the scope of the subject must be clearly defined. Also there will be no formal speeches, but if possible those taking part should be told in advance what the topic is to be so that they can prepare what they have to say and produce documentary and statistical evidence to support their arguments.

The chairman will be required to direct the course of the discussion, to confine the comments of speakers to the subject in hand, and perhaps from time to time to sum up the points made.

Debate

For a debate, it is necessary to appoint two speakers in addition to the chairman. Unlike an informal discussion, a debate must have a definite motion. This will be in the form of a statement which will be supported by the first speaker and opposed by the second.

For example, a suitable motion based on the first passage below might be:

This House believes that man can cope without recourse to God as a working hypothesis.

The chairman will open the debate by introducing the motion and inviting the proposer to speak first. The speeches of both the proposer and opposer should be subject to a time limit. If there are seconders to these speakers they should follow in the same order and be restricted to a shorter time than the first two speakers. After these prepared speeches, the chairman can open the discussion to the floor of the house for the other people present to express their opinions.

N.B. Remember that all remarks must be addressed directly to the chairman.

It is the duty of the chairman to curtail fruitless dispute and to concentrate the attention of all speakers on the motion under debate. He himself should not express personal opinions regarding the subject being discussed.

When the chairman considers that all profitable discussion is exhausted, he should call upon the opposer to sum up his case. The proposer has the privilege of speaking last in summing up his reasons for supporting the motion. After this, the chairman will read the motion again and put it to the vote. If necessary, he will appoint tellers to count the votes.

Some members of the group taking part can be asked to make notes of the debate in order to prepare a summary or minutes of the proceedings.

EXTRACTS FOR DISCUSSION

In the passages which follow, the writers take a particular stand and endeavour to support the case they are presenting. Where possible, analyse the prejudices of each in order to see how these have arisen and whether the attitudes are justifiable.

In order to make the maximum effect, these writers deliberately over-simplify the issues and at times go to extremes so that those who oppose their ideas will be roused into active disagreement. It is hoped that these extracts will create a healthy scepticism concerning matters over which we have perhaps become a little too complacent.

The questions which follow each passage are designed to stimulate discussion. Naturally other factors will arise from the passage and you are encouraged to take a wider view of each problem than that presented by the author.

1. The movement beginning about the thirteenth century towards the autonomy of man has in our time reached a certain completion. Man has learned to cope with all questions of importance without recourse to God as a working hypothesis. In questions concerning science, art, and even ethics, this has become an understood thing which one scarcely dares to tilt at any more. But for the last hundred years or so it has been increasingly true of religious questions also:

it is becoming evident that everything gets along without 'God', and just as well as before. As in the scientific field, so in human affairs generally, what we call 'God' is being more and more edged out of life, losing more and more ground.

Catholic and Protestant historians are agreed that it is in this development that the great defection from God, from Christ, is to be discerned, and the more they bring in and make use of God and Christ in opposition to this trend, the more the trend itself considers itself to be anti-Christian.

June 8th, 1944.
Letters and Papers from Prison, Dietrich Bonhoeffer.

(1) What evidence leads you to believe that 'Man has learned to cope with all questions of importance without recourse to God as a working hypothesis'?
(2) Do we suffer in any way from this 'defection from God'?
(3) Can Christianity survive if the traditional belief in God disappears?
(4) Do the teachings of Christ still have a validity in a world which has 'learned to cope without God'?
(5) Would you consider that Britain is no longer a Christian country?

2. Man is a machine, the brain secretes thought as the liver secretes bile. How simple it all was, how luminously obvious! With all the fervour of a convert at a revival meeting, he decided for atheism. In the circumstances it was only to be expected. You can't stomach St. Augustine any more, you can't go on repeating the Athanasian rigmarole. So you pull the plug and send them down the drain. What bliss! But not for very long. Something, you discover, is missing. The experimental baby was flushed out with the theological dirt and soapsuds. But nature abhors a vacuum. Bliss gives place to a chronic discomfort, and now you're afflicted, generation after generation, by a succession of Wesleys, Puseys, Moodies and Billies —Sunday and Graham—all working like beavers to pump the theology back out of the cesspool. They hope, of course, to recover the baby. But they never succeed. All that a revivalist can do is to siphon up a little of the dirty water. Which, in due course, has to be thrown out again. And so on indefinitely.

Island, Aldous Huxley.

(1) Is it distasteful to consider man as merely a machine?
(2) What is man besides being a machine?

(3) What is it that the atheist feels is missing when he rejects religious belief?
(4) What are your views on revivalists such as Billy Graham?

3. *Religious Summary*

It is time to tell our Fundamentalists bluntly that they are the worst enemies of religion today; that Jehova is no god, but a barbarous tribal idol; that the English Bible, though a masterpiece of literary art in its readable parts, and, being the work of many highly gifted authors and translators, rich in noble poems, proverbs, precepts, and entertaining if not always edifying stories, is yet a jumble of savage supersitition, obsolete cosmology, and a theology which, beginning with Calibanesque idolatory and propitiatory blood sacrifices (Genesis to Kings), recoils into sceptical disillusioned atheistical Pessimism (Ecclesiastes); revives in a transport of revolutionary ardour as the herald of divine justice and mercy and the repudiation of all sacrifices (Micah and the Prophets); relapses into sentimentality by conceiving God as an affectionate father (Jesus); reverts to blood sacrifices and takes refuge from politics in Other-Worldliness and Second Adventism (the Apostles); and finally explodes in a mystical opium dream of an impossible apocalypse (Revelations): every one of these phases being presented in such an unbalanced one-sided way, that the first Christian Catholic Church forbad the laity to read the Bible without special permission. When the Reformation let it loose on Mr. Everyman, it produced a series of wars of religion which have culminated today in the Hitlerized world war. In this the campaigns of Joshua for the conquest of his world have broken out again with the difference that the Germans and not the Jews are the Chosen Race (Herrenvolk) who are to conquer and inherit the earth; and the lands flowing with milk and honey which they are to invade and put to the sword are not only the patches of North Africa which used to be called the land of Canaan but virtually the whole five continents. It is one of the paradoxes of the situation that Joshua Hitler, born in comparative poverty into the bitter strife of petty commerce in which the successful competition of the Jews is specially dreaded and resented, and for which he is himself unfitted by his gifts, hates the Jews, and yet is so saturated by his early schooling with the Judaism of the Bible that he now persecutes the Jews even to extermination just as the first Joshua persecuted the Canaanites, and is leading his country to ruin not through anti-Semitism but through Bible Semitism with its head turned.

Yet from my reading aloud of all this writing on the wall, Mr. Everyman, who never reads the Bible, and never listens critically to the ritual of having the lessons read to him every Sunday in Church (when he goes to Church: a habit which he is dropping), gathers nothing but that I am a damnably irreligious man who will certainly go to hell when I die if there be any such place as hell, which Mr. Everyman is beginning to doubt, because it has uncomforting possibilities for himself as well as certainty for me.

Everybody's Political What's What? (1944), George Bernard Shaw.

(1) How seriously can we treat Shaw's judgements on the sections of the Bible he mentions?
(2) Can the Bible be considered purely as a work of history and literature?
(3) Is there any validity in Shaw's comparison of the Jews and the Germans as the 'Chosen Race'?
(4) What was the cause of Hitler's hatred of the Jews?
(5) If Mr. Everyman doubts the existence of hell, does he also doubt the existence of heaven?

4. 'You seem to have solved your economic problems pretty successfully.'

'Solving them wasn't difficult. To begin with, we never allowed ourselves to produce more children than we could feed, clothe, house, and educate into something like full humanity. Not being over-populated, we have plenty. But although we have plenty, we've managed to resist the temptation that the West has now succumbed to—the temptation to over-consume. We don't give ourselves coronaries by guzzling six times as much saturated fat as we need. We don't hypnotize ourselves into believing that two television sets will make us twice as happy as one television set. And finally we don't spend a quarter of the gross national product preparing for World War III or even World War's baby brother, Local War MMMCCXXXIII. Armaments, universal debt, and planned obsolescence—those are the three pillars of Western prosperity. If war, waste, and money lenders were abolished, you'd collapse. And while you people are over-consuming, the rest of the world sinks more and more deeply into chronic disaster. Ignorance, militarism, and breeding, these three—and the greatest of these is breeding. No hope, not the slightest possibility, of solving the economic problem until *that's* under control. As population rushes up, prosperity goes down.'

Island, Aldous Huxley.

(1) Can all economic problems be solved by birth control?
(2) In your opinion, has the West 'succumbed to the temptation to over-consume'?
(3) Do you agree that the three pillars of Western prosperity are 'Armaments, universal debt, and planned obsolescence'?
(4) Can we afford to reduce the country's spending on armaments?
(5) How far do you agree with this simple diagnosis of the diseases of Western civilization?

5. Two interesting facts emerge from an election day article on the Gallup poll. One is that because the names of the candidates' parties are not given on ballot-papers, up to three per cent of the votes are cast 'at random'. In other words, out of a total electorate of about 35 million, more than one million have only the haziest idea of whom they are voting for.

The other is that when asked in the latest poll which party they thought would win the election, one per cent of those questioned answered 'the Liberals'. In other words, there are about 500 000 voters in the country who either have an over-developed sense of humour, are mentally deficient or are completely out of touch with political realities.

Such are some of the absurd consequences of 'one-man-one-vote' democracy, a system which hardly anyone in this country dare openly question. It is a system which ensures that the ignorant and moronic have the same voice in choosing a Government as the educated and intelligent. What is this but political superstition?

The Daily Telegraph, 'Peter Simple'.

(1) What are the advantages of giving the candidate's political party on the ballot-paper?
(2) Are there reasons why the political party names ought *not* to appear on the ballot-paper?
(3) What are the 'absurd consequences' which arise from the one-man-one-vote democracy?
(4) How could such anomalies be overcome?
(5) Why does one hardly dare to question openly the one-man-one-vote democracy?

6. State welfare encourages the notion that 'the state' should provide, not the family or individuals; it has thus impoverished us by inciting us to beggar and demean one another. Doctors are mis-used for trifling ailments. Council houses are occupied by tenants who demand garages. Children who can support their parents throw them

on the state—in hospitals that become hostels. Students who demand higher grants to avoid dependence on their parents see nothing wrong in depending on other students' parents. Politicians who tell pensioners that a means test implies dependence on their children
10 see no wrong in keeping them dependent on other pensioners' children. We have all become accustomed to taking money—allowances, grants, 'insurance' benefits, pensions—we do not need (and have probably not paid for). But a society in which we are allowed or encouraged to get as much as we can from one another
15 does not foster self-respect or integrity.

State welfare has created 'topsy-turvy' scales of values. It is considered proper to spend money on the pleasurable—clothes, drinking, smoking, amusements, holidays—but not on essentials. A man who spends on education is accused of buying privilege, but
20 he is 'with it' if he spends lavishly on record-players, cars, a fortnight in Spain. Since private spending on welfare is socially ostracized and consumption socially approved, is it any wonder that so much advertising and productive resources are diverted from welfare to consumption?

Welfare by Choice (*Rebirth of Britain*), Arthur Seldon.

(1) In what respect has the welfare state in Britain gone too far?
(2) In what respect has the welfare state in Britain not gone far enough?
(3) Can personal responsibility be maintained when so many services are provided by the state?
(4) Should council house tenants demand garages?
(5) Do we spend too much money on luxuries instead of on essentials?
(6) Should a man be allowed to spend freely on private education?
(7) In which instances should private spending on welfare services be restored or restricted?

7. 'What right', they asked, 'has one man to wealth when another has none, what right has any man to rule over his brother? Is not inequality an affront to the dignity of man?' These notions were the pure milk of the gospel. So influential were they that many early
5 socialists were only won round to accept the need for the fullest opportunities for individual ascent by the brilliant invention of the idea of equality of opportunity. When opportunity was coupled with equality it was made more than respectable; it became the Holy Grail. Socialists did not see that, as it was applied in practice,

equality of opportunity meant equality of opportunity to be unequal. This structural blindness was necessary if the Socialists were to concentrate with vigour upon opening wide the doors to talent. In practice, as I mentioned earlier, they attacked with most energy the forms of inequality due to inheritance. Death duties, the decay of nepotism, free secondary and university education, the integration of the public schools, wages for children, the abolition of the hereditary House of Lords, these are their most momentous achievements.

The Rise of Meritocracy, Michael Young.

(1) Are there any circumstances where equality between men is not only impossible but undesirable?
(2) Does equality of opportunity mean equality of opportunity to be unequal?
(3) In what respect is inequality due to inheritance still evident?
(4) What case can you make for the retention of public schools?
(5) What case can you make for the retention of the House of Lords?

8. Were it announced tomorrow that anyone who fancied it might without risk of reprisals or recriminations, stand at a fourth-storey window, dangle out of it a length of string with a meal (labelled 'Free') on the end, wait till a chance passer-by took a bite and then, having entangled his cheek or gullet on a hook hidden in the food, haul him up to the fourth floor and there batter him to death with a knobkerrie, I do not think there would be many takers.

Most sane adults would, I imagine, sicken at the mere thought. Yet sane adults do the equivalent to fish every day: not in panic, sexual jealousy, ideological frenzy or even greed—many of our freshwater fish are virtually inedible, and not one of them constitutes a threat to the life, love or ideology of a human on the bank—but for amusement. Civilization is not outraged at their behaviour. On the contrary: that a person's hobby is fishing is often read as a guarantee of his sterling and innocent character.

The relationship of homo-sapiens to the other animals is one of unremitting exploitation. We employ their work; we eat and wear them. We exploit them to serve our superstitions: whereas we used to sacrifice them to our gods and tear out their entrails in order to

20 foresee the future, we now sacrifice them to science, and experiment on their entrails in the hope—or on the mere off-chance—that we might thereby see a little more clearly into the present. When we can think of no pretext for causing their death and no profit to turn it to, we often cause it none the less, wantonly, the only gain being a brief
25 pleasure for ourselves, which is usually only marginally bigger than the pleasure we could have had without killing anything; we could quite well enjoy marksmanship or cross-country galloping without requiring a real dead wild animal to show for it at the end.

It is rare for us to leave wild animals alive; when we do, we
30 often do not leave them wild. Some we put on display in a prison just large enough for them to survive, but not in any full sense to live in. Others we trundle about the country in their prisons, pausing every now and then to put them on public exhibition performing, like clockwork, 'tricks' we have 'trained' into them. However,
35 animals are not clockwork but instinctual beings. Circus 'tricks' are spectacular or risible as the case may be precisely because they violate the animals' instinctual nature—which is precisely why they ought to violate both our moral and our aesthetic sense.

But where animals are concerned humanity seems to have switched
40 off its morals and aesthetics—indeed, its very imagination. Goodness knows those faculties function erratically enough in our dealings with one another. But at least we recognise their faultiness. We spend an increasing number of our cooler moments trying to forestall the moral and aesthetic breakdowns which are liable, in a crisis, to
45 precipitate us into atrocities against one another. We have bitter demarcation disputes about where the rights of one man end and those of the next man begin but most men now acknowledge that there are such things as the rights of the next man. Only in relation to the next animal can civilised humans persuade themselves that
50 they have absolute and arbitrary rights—that they may do anything whatever that they can get away with.

The Sunday Times, Brigid Brophy.

(1) Would you support the writer's implication that fishing is a hobby for sadists? How would you defend angling against the charges she makes?
(2) Can experiments on animals be morally justifiable?
(3) Is hunting still possible as a sport 'without requiring a real dead wild animal to show for it at the end'?
(4) Do you consider that zoos and circuses cause unnecessary suffering to animals? Should they be abolished?

(5) Without being sentimental, do you agree with the writer's opinions? What actions can we take to remedy the situations described?

9. The thing in Ruth Harrison's book that has hurt farmers most is the accusation that modern stock-men, in contrast to their more worthy forefathers, are, if not actively cruel, at least callous and indifferent to their stock, and concerned only with making the maximum profit out of them without regard for their welfare. This, they feel, is grossly unfair. It shows that she lacks understanding both of how they regard their animals and of the nature of the animals themselves.

To most townswomen, I suppose, the word 'animals' means dogs or cats or budgies—individuals on which the owner and his family lavish considerable affection, and with which they have a strong, if usually one-sided, emotional relationship. Their idea of farm animals is based on this experience and, doubtless, tinged with memories from their childhood comics of jolly pigs in trousers called Porky Boy or Percy Pig. As Louis Golding wrote in 'Malabar Farm': 'The trouble with the animals in this family is that they think they're people.'

To the livestock farmer who works with his animals and makes his living from them this is sheer sentimental clap-trap. He is, I have no doubt, as fond of his sheep-dog as any other dog-owner (though he expects a sensible degree of discipline and a fair day's work from him); and he may say of an old cow, as she reaches the end of a long life of useful lactations, 'I shall miss old Daisy'. But where he is dealing with large numbers of animals, a flock of sheep or a battery-house full of hens, such feelings for individuals do not arise; and, in particular, where he is raising animals for eventual slaughter for meat they are unthinkable. What he does have is a strong feeling of obligation for their welfare: to provide the right kinds of food and living conditions in which they will flourish. His motive in this, it is true, may not aspire to great moral heights—only if they are well fed and comfortable will they yield him the profit he seeks—but the feeling of obligation is indisputably there and drives him to forgo personal comfort for their benefit; to struggle through snow and storm, if need be, to tend them. In this the modern farmer is no less conscientious than his forefathers.

Equally sentimental, to the farmer's mind, is the way people will insist on attributing human feelings to animals. Ruth Harrison, for instance, writes of depriving calves of the 'pleasure' of grazing, and battery hens of their 'freedom'. I have been studying wild animals and birds all my life and working closely with farm animals for twenty-five years, and I am convinced that to think in these terms is strictly nonsensical. Animals do not lead their lives on this level of self-consciousness. Their experiences are all immediate: heat, cold or a comfortable temperature; hunger or a satisfyingly full belly; fright, but not fear in the sense of foreboding; so that a calf or hen properly housed and fed is no more or less 'happy', feels no more or less 'pleasure', than if it were out of doors and running free.

Here is a fertile field for misunderstandings. If you think of animals as lesser projections of human beings, you will judge that confining them in cages or keeping them in semi-darkness is cruel, because you would not like it for yourself. If, on the other hand, you think of them as the animals they are and, in working with them daily, observe their behaviour and see that they are thriving and putting on weight or producing a lot of eggs or whatever it is you keep them for, you will make a very different judgement. These misunderstandings seem to me a pity, because they widen the gulf between town and country.

They also divert attention from some important problems that undoubtedly exist in the new intensive systems of keeping livestock. These problems are of even more concern to farmers than to others, because farmers' livelihoods depend on their solution. When animals are kept in large numbers close together, there are special risks of disease spreading among them. Much has still to be learnt about the safe use of antibiotics and hormones. As more productive breeds are developed, an increasing strain is put on their constitutions; the effects merit much study. Feeding for quick growth requires a very exact knowledge of nutrition, especially of the need for various amino-acids and vitamins. The problems are many.

But there have been problems ever since early man started to domesticate animals and keep them for his own use. Not least of those facing modern man is how to feed, and feed better, his own species whose numbers are increasing at an explosive rate. The efficient and economical conversion of cereals and grass products into animal protein can make a vital contribution to solving this.

R. K. Cornwallis, from *The Countryman.*

(1) Do you feel that the forced rearing and battery production of animals for food is cruel and callous? Have farmers looked for false excuses to explain their methods?

(2) Do townspeople have too sentimental and emotional an attitude towards animals?
(3) Is the farmer's concern for his animals purely financial?
(4) Are you convinced by the author's arguments in paragraph four regarding the feelings of animals?
(5) Is it morally justifiable to raise animals to be slaughtered for food?
(6) What reactions would Miss Brophy and Mr. Cornwallis have to each other's opinions about animals?

10. BUSINESSMEN PREFER TO BE SQUIRES
'DEEP-ROOTED SNOBBERY'

Forty £3,000-a-year British business executives were interviewed by a team of psychological research workers during a search for an incentive scheme to coax them to work harder.

But yesterday Mr. William Schlackman, 37, American-born head of the team said with shock that more than half had only one ambition: not to work at all.

'They would rather retire as gentleman-farmers if they had the means than end up as chairman of the group, in effect rating a sporting squire superior to a captain of industry', he went on.

'They aspired to part-time directorship so that work could become a hobby and their hobby, golf, their real work; perhaps with some social service as a magistrate or councillor thrown in, sanctified because it is unpaid.'

He had found a deep-rooted snobbery. There was:

An accountant who took two hours' work home each night, but insisted on arriving at his office an hour later than his staff to demonstrate his privilege of rank;

A research supervisor who was outraged when issued with a linen jacket to protect his suit from chemicals. 'What do they think I am, a lab assistant?' he asked;

A brilliant production manager, who was ashamed rather than proud to admit that he had worked his way up from the factory floor.

Three-quarters of the executives said they would rather be members of the House of Lords than of the Commons and generally tended to value status above power.

The Daily Telegraph.

(1) In your opinion is the attitude described characteristic of most British businessmen?

(2) Would you rather be a gentleman-farmer than a successful businessman?

(3) Why is it that British businessmen seem somewhat reluctant to become chairmen of companies?

(4) Is it morally wrong to have the sole ambition not to work at all?

(5) Why should three-quarters of the executives interviewed prefer to be members of the House of Lords than of the Commons?

(6) Should we consider seriously Mr. Schlackman's findings? Is it possible to trace a failure of higher management to the opinions he discovered?

11. The following figures indicate government spending in the United Kingdom in 1971

Social security benefits	£3,968m
Education	£2,703m
Health and Welfare	£2,559m
Defence	£2,514m
Housing	£1,244m
Roads	£812m
Overseas aid	£193m

If you were in a position to influence spending in these spheres, what alterations to the apportioning of these sums of money would you hope to make?

12. As the educational system produces more economists, economic crises become more acute; as a growing study is made of industrial relations, industrial disputes increase. What are the causes of this apparent paradox?

13. When the white man came to Africa, the white man had the Bible and the African had the land, but now it is the white man who is being, reluctantly and bloodily, separated from the land, and the African who is attempting to digest or to vomit up the Bible.

Down at the Cross, James Baldwin.

14. The shame of doing anything for which the neighbours could look down on one is a very powerful social force.

Juvenile Delinquency, A. E. Jones.

15. To me it seems that those who are happy in this world are better and more lovable people than those who are not.
                                      Samuel Butler.

16. All I know is that everything in a vague sort of way means something else, and I want desperately to find out what.
                                      Sidney Keyes.

17. I mistrust those banks. They do what they like. When I go into my bank somehow they make me feel as if I'd done something wrong, or at least I'd better mind what I was about: and they look at you superior as if you were asking a favour. Oh very polite, but so condescending.
                           Riceyman Steps, Arnold Bennett.

18. My longing is more and more for one thing only, integrity, and I discount the other qualities in people far too ruthlessly if they lack that fundamental sincerity and wholeness.
                                      Alun Lewis.

19. Extremism in the defence of liberty is no vice; Moderation in the pursuit of justice is no virtue.
                                Senator Barry Goldwater.

20. Genius—it is nothing but this, that a man knows what he can do best, and does it, and nothing else.
                                      Olive Schreiner.

Appendix I: Addresses of Examining Boards

Ordinary National Diploma and Ordinary National Certificate in Business Studies (Rule 124):

The Secretary, Joint Committee for National Awards in Business Studies and Public Administration, Department of Education and Science, Elizabeth House, York Road, London S.E.1. Tel. 01-928 9222.

Scottish National Certificate in Business Studies:

The Secretary, The Scottish Business Examinations Council (SCOTBEC), 22 Great King Street, Edinburgh EH3 6HQ. Tel. 031-556 4691.

Clerical Examination and Diploma in Public Administration:

The Local Government Examinations Board, 93 Albert Embankment, London S.E.1. Tel. 01-735 0191.

Shorthand Typist's Certificate:

The Royal Society of Arts, Examinations Board, 18 Adam Street, Adelphi, London WC2N 6AJ. Tel. 031-839 1691.

Private Secretary's Certificate and Private Secretary's Diploma:

The London Chamber of Commerce, Commercial Education Scheme, 109 Station Road, Sidcup, Kent DA15 7BJ. Tel. 01-302 0261-4.

Part I Examination:

The Institute of Bankers, 10 Lombard Street, London EC3V 9AS. Tel. 01-623 3531.

Intermediate Examination:

The Institute of Chartered Secretaries and Administrators: 16 Park Crescent, London W1N 4AH. Tel. 01-580 4741 and 01-580 1591.

Graduate Examination:

The Institute of Transport, 80 Portland Place, London W1N 4DP. Tel. 01-580 5216.

Intermediate Examination:

The Institute of Export, Export House, 14 Hallam Street, London W1N 6HT. Tel. 01-636 6761.

Foremanship and Supervision Examination:

City and Guild of London Institute, The National Examinations Board in Supervisory Studies, 76 Portland Place, London W1N 4DP. Tel. 01-580 3050.

Associate Examination Part 1:

The Savings Bank Institute, Knighton House, 52 Mortimer Street, London W.1. Tel. 01-580 0791.

Introductory Examination:

The Chartered Insurance Institute, 20 Aldermanbury, London EC2V 7HY. Tel. 01-606 3835.

Appendix II: Bibliography

The Concise Oxford Dictionary, 5th edition, Oxford University Press, 1964.
Roget's Thesaurus, Everyman, Longman or Penguin, 1970.
Fowler, H. W.: *Modern English Usage*, 2nd edition (ed. Gowers), Oxford University Press, 1965.
Gowers, Sir Ernest: *The Complete Plain Words*, H.M.S.O. or Penguin; revised edition, 1970.
A Guide to the Writing of Business Letters.
Report Writing.
Hours into Minutes, British Association for Commercial and Industrial Education, 1966
Anderson, C. R.: *Business Reports*, 3rd edition, McGraw-Hill, 1957.
Gartside, L. : *Modern Business Correspondence*, 2nd edition, MacDonald & Evans, 1967.
Jones, E.: *The Way to Write Successful Letters*, Allen & Unwin, 1962.
Stephenson, J.: *Principles and Practice of Commercial Correspondence*, 4th edition, Pitman.
Thouless, R. H.: *Straight and Crooked Thinking*, Pan, 1966; revised edition, 1970.

Printed in Great Britain at the Alden Press, Oxford